Developing Turn-Based Multiplayer Games

with GameMaker Studio 2 and NodeJS

Yadu Rajiv

Apress®

Developing Turn-Based Multiplayer Games

Yadu Rajiv
Bangalore, Karnataka, India

ISBN-13 (pbk): 978-1-4842-3860-8 ISBN-13 (electronic): 978-1-4842-3861-5
https://doi.org/10.1007/978-1-4842-3861-5

Library of Congress Control Number: 2018964003

Managing Director, Apress Media LLC: Welmoed Spahr
Acquisitions Editor: Nikhil Karkal
Development Editor: Matthew Moodie
Coordinating Editor: Divya Modi

Cover designed by eStudioCalamar
Cover image designed by Freepik (www.freepik.com)

Distributed to the book trade worldwide by Springer Science+Business Media New York, 233 Spring Street, 6th Floor, New York, NY 10013. Phone 1-800-SPRINGER, fax (201) 348-4505, e-mail orders-ny@springer-sbm.com, or visit www.springeronline.com. Apress Media, LLC is a California LLC and the sole member (owner) is Springer Science + Business Media Finance Inc (SSBM Finance Inc). SSBM Finance Inc is a **Delaware** corporation.

For information on translations, please e-mail rights@apress.com, or visit http://www.apress.com/rights-permissions.

Apress titles may be purchased in bulk for academic, corporate, or promotional use. eBook versions and licenses are also available for most titles. For more information, reference our Print and eBook Bulk Sales web page at http://www.apress.com/bulk-sales.

Any source code or other supplementary material referenced by the author in this book is available to readers on GitHub via the book's product page, located at www.apress.com/978-1-4842-3860-8. For more detailed information, please visit http://www.apress.com/source-code.

Printed on acid-free paper

To my wife, Pooja, for all the love, courage, and strength that keeps me going; and to our lovely daughter Leela, who keeps us on our toes. To my father, mother, and brother for their love and unwavering support.

Table of Contents

About the Author

Yadu Rajiv is a Game Designer, Developer, curator, and evangelist for independent games. In 2011, he co-founded Hashstash Studios, where he designed and developed multiple games. He teaches User Experience Design, Game Design, and Game Development at Srishti Institute of Art, Design and Technology, Bangalore, India. He has been building and supporting communities around game design and development since 2008 and is currently working on GameDev.in (`http://gamedev.in`). Yadu writes about Game Design, Game UX, and Development on Twitter under his handle, yadurajiv, as well as on his blog (`http://yadurajiv.com`).

About the Technical Reviewer

 **Dickson Law** is a GameMaker hobbyist, commentator, and extension developer with 8 years of community experience. In his spare time, he enjoys writing general-purpose libraries, tools, and articles covering basic techniques for GameMaker Studio. As a web programmer by day, his main areas of interest include integration with server-side scripting and API design. He lives in Toronto, Canada.

Acknowledgments

First, I want to thank my wife, Pooja, and our beautiful baby girl Leela. You have given me the strength and courage to keep myself afloat and sail on through the storms to find my small island of creativity.

I'd also like to thank my Acquisitions Editor at Apress, Nikhil Karkal, for having faith in me and signing me up to write this book and my Coordinating Editor, Divya Modi, for her immense patience and constant support. Huge thanks to Matthew Moodie and Dickson Law for doing the technical review and weighing in at the right places to help me shape the content accurately.

I want to thank my friends Joel, Rishi, and Kinshuk for being constant forces of positive encouragement in my life.

A big shoutout to the community of game developers in Bangalore and the whole of India, and to all the Indies who keep the dream alive!

Lastly, I want to thank you, the reader, for buying this book. I hope it helps you get started on the extraordinary journey that is gamedev.

Introduction

Welcome to *Developing Turn-Based Multiplayer Games with GameMaker Studio 2 and Node.js*. This book will serve as a quick introduction to making turn-based multiplayer games with GameMaker Studio 2.

This book will serve as a handy guide to those who are already familiar with GameMaker Studio as well as an introduction to those who are new to it.

The first two chapters of the book introduce you to GameMaker Studio and how to start working with GameMaker Language (GML). We reinforce your learning in Chapter 3 by making a simple, well-rounded, and playable game.

Chapter 4 focuses on setting up and getting started with Node.js and writing a simple server. Chapter 5 builds upon this experience to write a simple dice roller server application that can communicate back and forth with a client game made in GameMaker Studio.

Chapter 6 focuses on taking you through the steps of building a slightly more complex turn-based game with Node.js.

Resources

The resources for this book can be downloaded via the download link provided here www.apress.com/978-1-4842-3860-8. This includes code and resources that are referred to in the following chapters.

CHAPTER 1

An Introduction to GMS2

In this chapter, you will get started with GameMaker Studio 2 (GMS2). The first thing we will be doing is to find out how we can download and install the latest version of GameMaker Studio 2. Once we have downloaded and installed the software, we will get started with an overview of GameMaker Studio 2's interface and then move on to create our first project.

Through this chapter, you will get a basic understanding of how a GameMaker Studio 2 project is laid out and navigate the integrated development environment (IDE). This will give you a foundation for all future projects to come.

Installing GameMaker Studio 2

Welcome to the exciting world of GameMaker Studio 2; I know that you are raring to go, but before we can do anything, we need to get ourselves a copy of GameMaker Studio 2. The easiest way of doing this is to go to the YoYo Games website and click on the button titled "Get GameMaker" (https://www.yoyogames.com/get).

This page displays various options for you to choose from, the first of them being the trial for GameMaker Studio 2. If you choose to go for the trial, you will be navigated to another page that prompts you to login or

© Yadu Rajiv 2018
Y. Rajiv, *Developing Turn-Based Multiplayer Games*,
https://doi.org/10.1007/978-1-4842-3861-5_1

register a new account with YoYo games. Once you register, you will receive an e-mail prompting you to reset your password, and once you are logged in, you are redirected to your My Accounts page, which gives you the option to download the Limited Trial version of GameMaker Studio 2 for both Windows and Mac. Click the Download GameMaker Studio 2 button to start your download.

If you scroll down, you will see options to purchase the full Desktop version and other modules that you will use to export your games to other platforms. Scroll down further and you will notice a table that lists the licenses available to you. By default, you have the GameMaker Studio 2 Trial license associated with your account.

Once the download completes, run the installer to install GameMaker Studio 2.

Once installed, click on the new GMS2 icon on your desktop to run it. You will be required to key in your e-mail and password for your YoYo Games account that you have previously created while GMS2 starts up for the first time. After you are successfully logged in and the application starts, you will be greeted by the Start Page and the Welcome page—both of which are accessible via the Help menu. The Welcome page gives you access to videos that can get you started with the key concepts behind GMS2 as well as what is new in GMS2 compared to its predecessor.

The Start page is divided into three parts. The top section contains links to recent blog posts, tutorials, and news from YoYo Games as well as links to demos you may have downloaded. The bottom half of the start page has is divided into two parts: on the left you have a list of recently accessed projects, and on the right, you have actions that you can perform. The Getting Started section includes options to create a new project, open an existing project, or import an existing GM:S 1.4 project. Below the Getting Started section, the Explore section provides links to the Marketplace as well as official YoYo Games GMS2 tutorials and projects that demonstrate specific features of GMS2 via demos.

Figure 1-1. *TheWelcome page and the Start page(first tab, hidden here)*

Tip   Detailed help is available to you at the click of a button, and that magic button is F1.

GameMaker Studio 2: An Overview

GameMaker Studio is a very structured piece of software. The tool tries to be a one-stop shop for all your 2D game development needs, and it does a pretty good job at it. Before getting started, it would be good to have a better understanding of the bigger picture.

The Resources Panel

Most of GameMaker Studio's workflow is centered around the resources you add into the program. The resource panel is a central part of almost everything you do in any GameMaker Project. It allows you to create, organize, and edit all the resources that your project will have. The most

3

common resources you will be using are Rooms, Sprites, Objects, Sounds, Scripts, and Fonts. There are more resources that you will work with, but you can make a functional game even with just these resources.

Rooms

Rooms are where your games happen; a room is a way of structuring different parts of your game. Rooms are equivalent to scenes in a film. You could have a room for your company logos, your main menu, level selection, levels, etc. A room is the only resource that is created for you by default when you start any new project. The first room at the top of the Rooms list is considered the entry point into your game. Everything pertaining to the room can be edited in the Room editor. The first room's size is taken into consideration when creating the application window. You must have at least one room in your project. Rooms have layers of different kinds—each layer is, in a way, specific to the kind of asset it can hold or a specific function it provides. The different kinds of layers are background, instance, tile, path, and asset. You can have more than one of these layers.

- **Background Layer**: This background layer essentially lets you pick a background color or a sprite; it also automatically tiles images and scrolls them to a set speed.

- **Instance Layer**: This is where all instances of the objects you created will go. This is one of the most commonly used layers. Almost all items we add to the game will go here.

- **Tile Layer**: This layer lets you create tile maps easily from a tile set. A tile set is a set of images, and a tile map is a large map created by placing these smaller tiles from the tile set.

- **Path Layer**: This is special layer that can hold Paths that has been created in the Resource panel. A path, which can be straight or curved, is formed of a list of connected points and is essentially used as a way for objects to move along it.

- **Asset Layer**: The asset layer lets you directly place or paint sprites into it.

Objects and Instances

Objects are our bread and butter. Objects are the building blocks of your game. They add the interactivity and logic that is at the core of every game. Objects have many properties—they can be visually represented through sprites, or they can exist without any other supporting resource, but they can receive and respond to events if they are placed inside a room. Objects need to be placed into rooms via the Room editor. When your game is executed, GameMaker creates the room and then goes on to create each layer and item on it. Each object in that room is an instance of that object.

Listening to Events

At its core, GameMaker Studio is event-driven; everything that happens in a game is a response to some sort of an event happening. They can be as generic as a Step event (an event that happens every frame of the game) or specific like a Mouse event on an instance of an object. GameMaker Studio expects you to build working systems and rules on top of these events and the information that GMS itself provides.

Starting Our First Project

When you click the Create New Project option on the Start Page or via the
File menu, you are given an option to switch between Drag and Drop and
GameMaker Language. The Drag and Drop option is a friendlier visual
interface for coding in the GameMaker Language, or GML for short.

The GML is the scripting language for GameMaker Studio. It shares
similarities with many languages like Lua, JavaScript, and C. Although the
language offers different styles of writing code, we will try to stick to one
style consistently across this book.

Starting off your adventures in GameMaker Studio using the Drag and
Drop will help you to get acquainted with GameMaker and programming
in GML. The GameMaker Language option lets you type in code directly
without the Drag and Drop interface. You can, however, alternate between
the two to an extent, as you will see in the future chapters. Let's focus on
how to get acquainted with coding from the get go. This chapter will ease
you into the programming interface that we will be using extensively in the
chapters to come. Click on GameMaker Language to continue.

You will be prompted with a save dialog box, which lets you save the
new project that you have started. Once saved, GMS2 greets you with an
empty workspace.

Figure 1-2. *A new project with an empty workspace*

At this point, you have a very rudimentary base game. Let's run this game and see what happens!

Figure 1-3. *The menu and toolbar-the Run button is the seventh from the left and looks like a Play button*

To run this base project of yours, you can use the Run button (as seen in Figure 1-3) from the main toolbar, select the Run command from the Build menu in the menu bar, or hit the F5 key. Once you hit Run, you would see a set of new windows appear near the bottom of the screen with a flurry of activity. The window that has focus is called the Output window. This window is one of the primary ways in which GameMaker Studio talks to you—about what it is currently doing, what has transpired, or when it encounters errors. This Output window is also a handy space for your game to send messages to as well. Once GMS2 compiles the project, it executes it, and now you should see a window with a black background.

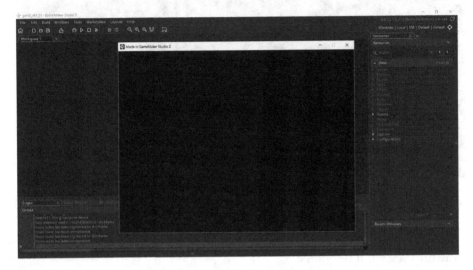

Figure 1-4. *Running your project for the first time*

Editing Our Rooms

On the left side you have your empty workspace, and on the right side you have your Resources panel, and docked within it your Recent windows panel as well. The Resource window contains all the elements pertaining to your project.

When you previously ran the game project via the Run command, you saw a black screen; this black and empty space was an empty room that was created for you by GameMaker Studio when it created the project for you.

Figure 1-5. *The room editor*

If you look at your resources panel on the right, you will see that there is a section called *Rooms* within it. Click this to see a list of rooms available to you. The list contains one room called *room0*. Let us try to edit this room; we can do this by double-clicking the room in the resources list. The room editor opens with a new panel to your left and the room now in the center. The left panel contains three sections that we will be using a lot: the first section is dedicated to layers in the room; the second portion is a context-sensitive panel dedicated to the properties of each of the selected layer; and the third section is dedicated to the properties (metadata/features) of the room.

Looking at the Room Settings in the Properties panel for the room, you can see that our room has a width and a height of 1024 and 768 pixels, respectively. Let us change it to 640 and 480 pixels and run the game after to see what happens. As you would have noticed, as we changed the size of the room, the room that was open in the middle also changed in size. When we run the game, the new window that is created will now become smaller in size. Let's change one more property—click on Backgrounds in the list of layers for this room in the Layers panel. The Background layer is a special layer that can act as a static or animated backdrop for the room. It can have a color or it can be a sprite (a sprite is the gamedev way of describing a static or animated image; we will look at sprites in detailed in upcoming chapters). For now, we will just change the color by clicking the dark bar labeled color. In the color picker that opens, select a color; I have set mine to white. Let's run the game again to see how it has changed.

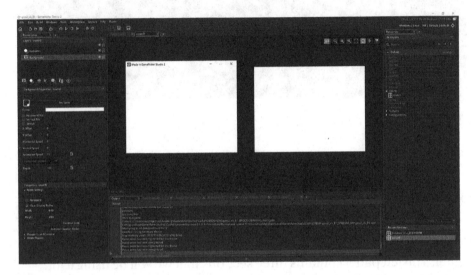

Figure 1-6. *The room with a new background color and new size. To view up to this point in the project, please open the file (gms2_ch_01_01.yyz).*

Now that we learned to edit the room and have a basic understanding of how the GMS2 interface works, lets jump in and explore the rest of GMS2 and how you can make your game come to life through the GML. To view our progress up to this point in the project, please open the file gms2_ch_01_01.yyz.

CHAPTER 2

An Introduction to GML

The GameMaker Language (GML) is what gives your games life and makes them tick. In this chapter we will learn about how to get started writing GML code, the basic structure, and flow of the language itself. There are two ways for writing GML in GameMaker Studio 2: one follows the traditional way of typing in the code into an editor space and the second uses the drag and drop method. We will forgo the drag and drop method in the interest of time as well as clarity when our code becomes slightly larger in scope.

Where to Write Code and What It Means

In GameMaker Studio 2 all the code we write gets compiled by the compiler before being executed. The compiler, in the simplest of terms, is a program that converts or translates the code you write into a language the computer can understand. By default you will be using the built-in virtual machine (VM) to test your game by simply pressing the Play button from the toolbar. You can also target the YoYo Compiler (YYC) or JavaScript for the HTML 5 target platform.

© Yadu Rajiv 2018
Y. Rajiv, *Developing Turn-Based Multiplayer Games,*
https://doi.org/10.1007/978-1-4842-3861-5_2

The VM output uses a generic runner (an application that loads and runs your game assets and code) for each target platform that interprets the compiled code. It is used mostly for smaller games or when performance is not a key factor. The YYC output compiles your code into native code that can run on the targeted platforms, unlike the VM, which acts as an intermediary. The YYC is heavily optimized and has enhanced performance but has higher compile times when compared to the VM.

You can find out more about compiling in the GMS2 documentation – (https://docs2.yoyogames.com/source/_build/1_overview/2_quick_start/6_compiling.html).

Events are fired by GMS2 when something specific happens; for example, when a user moves their mouse over an object, the mouse-enter event for that object is fired, likewise when the user clicks and releases their left mouse button, multiple events are fired in succession—a mouse left-down event, a mouse left-pressed event, and a mouse left-released event, to name a few. We can listen for these events and act accordingly when they are fired. Only objects have the capability to listen to all events—these can be events associated with that object and its instance, or they can be global events associated with input, networks, rooms, etc.

Instances of objects placed in rooms have some properties that we can edit individually in the Instance Editor. One such special property that can be edited is the *Creation Code* section. The code in the *Creation Code* event is executed right after the object's Create event. Here we will be able to manipulate specific properties pertaining to that instance of the object. Similarly, the Room resource also has a *Creation Code* event. When the Room is created, code in the *Creation Code* event for the room is executed.

With all these events available, there will be times when you would want to know the exact order in which these events are executed. We are unable to clearly determine the exact order in which events are executed during each frame of the game, but we can be sure of certain events that always run in the same order. Let's look at the first set of events that are fired and the order in which they are fired.

1. **Object Variables**: The object variables are the first to be set when a room is entered. Object variables are those defined via the Object Editor.

2. **Instance Variables**: If you override any of those Object Variables in the instances via the Room Editor, those will get set next.

3. **Create Event**: After this, the Create event for each object is called.

4. **Instance Creation Code**: The Create event is followed by the instance's creation code.

5. **Game Start Event**: If the Object has a Game Start event, then this is called next.

6. **Room Creation Code**: After the Game Start event, the code in the Room Creation Section for the room is executed.

7. **Room Start Event**: Finally, the Room Start event for the Object is called.

Apart from these events, the Step and Draw events of objects are also executed in a set order. The Step events in an object occur in the following order:

1. **Begin Step Event**: Executed first before the Step event

2. **Step Event**: The actual step event, executed before objects are moved to new positions, if any

3. **End Step Event**: Executed after the Step event

The Draw events execution order is as follows:

1. **Pre-Draw Event**: Executed first, before all other Draw events

2. **Draw Begin Event**: Executed right before the Draw event

3. **Draw Event**: The actual Draw event

4. **Draw End Event**: Executed after the Draw event

5. **Post-Draw Event**: Wrapping up the Draw events with the post-draw event

6. **Draw GUI Begin Event**: Once all other game elements are drawn, the Draw GUI Begin gets triggered.

7. **Draw GUI Event**: Then the actual Draw GUI event occurs.

8. **Draw GUI End Event**: The Draw GUI End event occurs last.

For more information regarding the Event Order, please visit the documentation (`https://docs2.yoyogames.com/source/_build/2_interface/1_editors/events/index.html#object_event_order`).

Apart from events, the other place where we will write code is using the Script Editor. We can directly add a Script resource and then have access to it via its name, like a function.

Let's create a small project to go over the points we have just discussed. When starting our new game project, we will pick GML instead of Drag and Drop. Once you have the new project up and running, right-click on Objects in the Resources Panel and select Create Object.

A new object called object0 will get added, and it will open in the Object Editor. In the Object Editor, click on the Add Event Button and select Create. In the Script Editor that opens, on the third line, type the following:

```
show_debug_message("Hello, I am making games!");
```

Once done, go back to the room, and then from the Resources Panel, drag and drop our new object0 into the room. After adding the object, run the game. Once the game executes, you should be able to see your message in the Output window in the GameMaker Studio IDE.

show_debug_message() is a built-in function. A function is a set of statements together that does something specific. In this case, this function displays a message you send to it. You passed the message, "Hello, I am making games!" as a parameter to the function. Depending on their use, some functions can require you to pass parameters, while sometimes others require none. We will explore when we create our own scripts later.

Even if the instance of our object is invisible, it is still part of the room; and the Create event was executed when the instance of the object was created. Now double-click on the instance of our object named *object0* from within the room editor to bring up the Instance Editor. In the Instance Editor, click on the *Creation Code* button to bring up the Script Editor. Add the following line to the *Creation Code* event:

```
show_debug_message("I am an instance of object0");
```

Run the program again to see what results you get. You will notice that our first message is displayed first, followed by the message from the instance creation code. Now let's try to add creation code to the room. Double-click the room in the Resources Panel and in the Room Editor, click the *Creation Code* button in the Properties panel to the left. In the Script Editor that opens, key in the following:

```
show_debug_message("Welcome to the room!");
```

Running the game now will show that the room's *Creation Code* is executed at the end after the object's *Create* event is fired and after the instance's *Creation Code* is executed.

Finally, let's create a script. We can do this by right-clicking on the Script section in the Resources Panel and selecting Create Script. As soon as the script is created, we have the option to rename it: we'll call our first script welcomeScript. Once this is done, click inside the Script Editor that is open in front of you. As you can see, the Script Editor's tab now says welcomeScript.gml. Script resources are saved on the disk and can be accessed outside of the GMS2 project as well. Scripts are usually used to store generic, often repeated, but useful functionality in a reusable manner. They can also be used to make your code cleaner and organized. Type the following in the Script Editor:

```
show_debug_message("Welcome to GameMaker Language! Have fun coding!");
```

Now to execute this script, let's go back to the Object Editor and select its Create event. Right above where were we wrote the code before, add in

```
welcomeScript();
show_debug_message("Hello, I am making games!");
```

Execute the game, and you should see the result shown in Figure 2-1.

Figure 2-1. *Output window with our debug messages*

First when the object was created and the Create event of the object was fired, we called our `welcomeScript` function/script. Then we printed out another message from the same event. Then we executed the commands in the instance's creation code as well as the room's creation code.

Commenting Your Code

Commenting on code is a way to annotate your code for clarity. When you create larger games, the amount of code and scripts that you use would need to manage usually increases exponentially. Comments serve to help you understand quickly what a chunk of code is intended to do. This comes in handy when you revisit sections of code after long intervals or act as helpful notes for other members of the team who would need to work with you. There are primarily two ways of commenting in GameMaker Studio: a single line comment and the multiline comment. Comments are ignored by the compiler, and you can write anything in them. Listing 2-1 below shows you how a single line comment works.

Listing 2-1. Single-Line Comment Describing the Actions in the Statements That Follows

```
// updates the player position
x += speedx * dt;
y += speedy * dt
```

Multiline comments function like single-line comments but can encompass a larger area. They also have a starting and an ending block. Anything after the first /* and before the */ is treated as a comment and ignored by the compiler. Listing 2-2 below shows you how multiline comments work.

Listing 2-2. Multiline Comments in Action

```
/*
To find the column without the % modulo operator
column = index - (row * width)
*/
column = index % width;
row    =  floor(index / width);

/*
show_debug_message(row);
show_debug_message(column);
*/
```

Here the first comment gives some information about the code below it, while the second comment helps to tell the compiler to ignore a set of actual code that would otherwise print the output to the console. Commenting large chunks of code, especially in larger projects in production, can cause more confusion than good. Aside from testing, commenting large sections of code is a bad practice and should be avoided.

GameMaker Studio also supports JSDoc style comments when it comes to commenting on parts of custom scripts. This will be explained when we start writing our own custom scripts.

Variables and Data

Variables are what we as well as GameMaker Studio use to store data. They can be numbers, text, true or false values, images, objects, collections of items, and much more. There are different kinds of variables in GMS—ones that are available to you globally and give you information about the system and the game itself and others that are contextual that give you information that is immediately related to where you are accessing the variable from. Apart from all these, there are variables that you create to store and manipulate different kinds of data. Let's go ahead and create an object and see what kinds of variables are available to us and what we can do with them.

Add a new object into the Objects section in the Resources Panel. Drag and add it into the room, and then open the Object from the Resources Panel in the Object Editor. Once it is open, click the Events button and add a Create event. Add the code shown in Listing 2-3 into the Create event. Let's try to print to the debug console the data that is contained in some of the built-in variables that we can use in the future.

Listing 2-3. Printing Some Built-In Variables to the Console (Refer to: gms2_ch02_01.yyz)

```
/// working with variables
// some properties of the room
show_debug_message(room_height);
show_debug_message(room_width);

// some properties of the object
show_debug_message(x);
show_debug_message(y);
```

When you check the console, you will see the width of your room and the height of your room printed one after the other as well as the x- and y-coordinate of our object in the room. If you don't see anything, make sure you placed an instance of the object in the room by dragging and dropping it. The first two are built-in properties of the room, and the x and y variables are built-in properties for the object. Move the instance around the room to a different position and see what values you get.

Not only can you read values, most of the values that are stored in the variables can be changed. Let's create a sprite from the sprite section in the Resources Panel and attach it to our object. Once you create a sprite, it opens in the Sprite Editor; for now, let's just edit the image by clicking the Edit Image button and give it a solid fill. Open the object in the Object Editor by double-clicking on it. Select the sprite you have just created in the sprite section of the Object Editor.

Let's change the x- and y-property of our object. Create a new event for the object and select the Step event. We will use the assignment operator = to set the values for the x and y variables. Let's set the x- and y-values to the mouse x- and mouse y-values, respectively (Listing 2-4).

Listing 2-4. Set the x- and y-Value of the Object to That of the x- and y-Values for the Mouse Cursor Position

```
x = mouse_x;
y = mouse_y;
```

When you run the game, you can see that now the object we have created follows the mouse wherever it goes. The mouse_x and mouse_y built-in variables contain the mouse position.

Since we have a sprite attached to the object, we can manipulate the sprite's properties as well. Let's try to change the rotation of the sprite every frame by adding this to the Step event. Run the game to see what happens, as in Listing 2-5.

Listing 2-5. Rotate the sprite 1 Degree Every Frame

```
image_angle = image_angle + 1
```

Instance, Local, and Global Variables

We saw some of the built-in variables which we have access to in action in the previous section. Here, we will look at instance, local, and global variables. Declaring and initializing an **instance variable** in GameMaker Studio is as easy as assigning a value to the variable name (see Listing 2-6).

Listing 2-6. Stores the String "Hello" in the Variable Message

```
message = "Hello";
```

As we have seen, most of the code you write is associated with objects or is in scripts. When you declare and initialize a variable like you see above, that variable has a scope within that object and its instances. You will constantly use them, as they can also be used across events and from other objects and instances. If you declare a variable in any event it becomes part of that object. Variables like these can be used to extend objects with custom properties, and it is good practice to declare and initialize them in the Create event. Trying to access variables that have not been declared will lead to errors, and those that are not initialized with any data may work in unpredictable ways. Instance variables for an instance will remain in memory till that instance is destroyed.

Listing 2-7. Extending a Player Object With Some Properties

```
playerMana = 10;
playerHealth = 100;
playerAttack = 5;
```

Local variables are like instance variables, but their scope is limited to the events in which they are declared. They are discarded and removed from memory as soon as the event is done. Because of their temporary nature, you will use them to do quick operations where you do not need to store data permanently or for a longer duration of time. You declare a local variable by using the var keyword before the variable name (see Listing 2-8).

Listing 2-8. Both Message and Length variables Will Be Discarded Once the Event/Script has Finished Executing

```
var message;
message = "hello friends!";
var length = string_length(message);
```

Global variables are variables that are persistent across instances, rooms, and scripts. Once declared they remain in memory and can be accessed anywhere until the end of the game. Global variables are useful to hold and manipulate information across instances, scripts and rooms. A great place to declare your global variables would be the start of the game. All global variables are declared as part of a constant called global. The variable you want to declare is added to this using a dot operator (see Listing 2-9).

Listing 2-9. A Global Variable Called currentLevel

```
global.currentLevel = 0;
```

We can manipulate this variable just as easily from anywhere. This is a blessing and a curse. If you are not extra careful when creating and manipulating global variables, they can cause serious problems in your game that can be very hard to track down and fix.

Listing 2-10. Incrementing the Global Variable

```
global.currentLevel = global.currentLevel + 1;
```

Accessing Variables From Other Instances

Instance variables can be accessed from other instances in two ways: one using the dot operator and the other using the with statement. There are different implications that one needs to be aware of while using these. You can access all instances and their variables in a room by using their object's name, which means if you have 10 instances of the object objEnemy, you can manipulate all of them by using the variable objEnemy. This is one of the features that make GameMaker Studio very powerful. Let's do a small exercise to see how this works (see Listing 2-11). Start by creating a new object called objEnemy and add a color variable to it in the Create event.

Listing 2-11. Our Enemy Is Yellow for Now

```
enemyColor = c_yellow;
```

Let's make the enemy visible by giving it a shape. Add a draw event to your enemy object and add the code from Listing 2-12 to it.

Listing 2-12. Draw a Circle With Our Enemy's Color

```
draw_set_color(enemyColor);
draw_circle(x,y, 10, false);
```

Drag and drop 10 of objEnemy objects onto the room, and run the game to see all of them being drawn on the screen. Once this is done, let's see how the dot operator and the with statement works. Create a new object and rename it objEnemyColorRandomize. Create a new rectangular sprite and add it to this object. Add a new Mouse-Left Released event to this object and add the following code to it (see Listing 2-13). Once this is done, drag and drop it to the middle of the room.

Listing 2-13. Change the Value of enemyColor in Each Instance to a Random Color

```
with(objEnemy) {
        enemyColor = make_color_hsv(irandom_range(0,255), 200,200);
}
```

The with statement in this case loops through all the instances of the object called objEnemy and changes the enemyColor variable to a random color.

Listing 2-14. Change the Value of enemyColor to One Random Color (gms2_ch02_02.yyz)

```
objEnemy.enemyColor = make_color_hsv(irandom_range(0,255),
200,200);
```

The primary difference is that the with operator works like a loop; it technically changes the current scope to that of the instance and then executes the statements within the brackets, whereas the dot directly sets the value that is assigned to all instances (see Listing 2-14). So, in the second case, we set a single randomly generated color to all the instances. We will explore the use of the with statement and the dot as we move forward. Do try both these statements to see how they differ from each other.

Instance-Related Keywords: Other, All, and No One

The other keyword is primarily used in two contexts: within a collision event, where the other refers to the other instance that collided with the calling instance and when using the with statement. We discussed that the with statement temporarily changes the scope to that of the given instance, and when, within that scope, you want to access data from the calling instance, you will need to use the other keyword. Let's rewrite our previous example to show you how the other keyword works (see Listing 2-15).

Listing 2-15. Accessing the Calling Instance's Variable Using the Other Keyword

```
color = make_color_hsv(irandom_range(0,255), 200,200);
with(objEnemy) {
        enemyColor = other.color;
}
```

Here, we define a variable color and create a random color value. Since we change the scope of an instance of objEnemy using the with statement, we use the other keyword to access the variable in the calling instance.

The all keyword is a special keyword that refers to all the active instances in the room. This can be used like the other keyword, especially with the with statement.

Tip   To know more about the with statement, select the word 'with' in your code and hit F1, and it will open the documentation on all language features in the GML.

The *no one* keyword is usually used to designate that the variable holds no instance. It is used widely to check if a variable holds some instance. In the following example, the instance_position function returns an id of an instance of the object objEnemy if it exists at the location mouse_x and mouse_y. If the object doesn't exist at that location, "noone" is returned.

```
var foundEnemy = instance_position( mouse_x, mouse_y,
objEnemy);
if(foundEnemy != noone) {
        instance_destroy(foundEnemy);
}
```

Operations Using Operators

We saw the assignment operator in action while accessing assigning values to variables and changing them. In this section we will go through some of the most common operators in GameMaker Studio.

Your basic arithmetical operators are +, -, *, and /, which do addition, subtraction, multiplication, and division, respectively. Listing 2-16 provides an examples of these.

Listing 2-16. Basic Arithmetical Operators in Action

```
sum = 5 + 10;
largeSum = sum * 15;
split = largeSum / 4;
```

Some of these operations can be written in short-hand using ++ and - - for addition and subtraction, respectively.

```
sum = sum + 1;
```

is the same as

```
sum++
```

Similarly, division can be rewritten with the keyword div. So, rewriting our earlier examples, we get the following:

```
split = largeSum div 4;
```

GameMaker Studio also has a handy modulo operator that gives you the remainder after division between two numbers. The modulo operator is represented by the % symbol or can be written as mod.

```
r = largeSum % 4;
```

We will return to look at more operators in the next section when we deal with control flow.

Managing Control Flow

A control flow statement is a set of statements that dictate how, what, and when parts of your code should be executed. By default, the flow of all code that is executed is from the top to the bottom and executed line by line. These statements help you to dictate what happens to this flow.

The if ... else if ... else Statement

You use the if statement to check if a specific condition has been met and, if so, then do some actions; if those conditions weren't met, do some other actions. The basic structure of the if statement is shown in Listing 2-17.

Listing 2-17. The sturcutre of the if...else if...else statement

```
if(condition) {
        // execute this if condition is met
} else if(another_condition) {
        // first condition not met, another_condition met
} else {
        // condition has not been met, execute this section
}
```

It also works in conjunction with a set of comparison, combining, and unary operators. Let's look at each of them using a small example.

In our example, we will make a small object with a sprite and move it on the screen using the keyboard keys. This time around, we will use only a Step event and the if statement. Start by creating a new project, adding an object and creating a small 64px × 64px sprite for the object. Drag and drop the object into the room and then add a Step event to the object from the Object Editor. Before we start off, let's write a bit of Pseudocode to describe what we are about to do (see Listing 2-18). Pseudocode is a way of describing an algorithm or the steps involved in a computer program at a higher level. It borrows the lingo and structures of a programming language but is written in human readable form for people to understand how a program or piece of code works.

Listing 2-18. Pseudo Code for What We Are Trying to Achieve

```
If the up arrow is pressed, then
        Move object one pixel to the up.
Else if the down arrow is pressed, then
        Move object one pixel to the down.

If the left arrow is pressed, then
        Move object one pixel to the left.
Else if the right arrow is pressed, then
        Move object one pixel to the right.
```

We want our object to move when we press our four arrow keys in each of those directions. We will use a built-in utility function keyboard_ check( ) to see if the arrow keys are being held down. The keyboard_ check( ) function takes in one parameter that represents the key we are checking for. To make our lives easier, GameMaker Studio has built in constants that we can use for the keys we need. In our Step event, write the code from Listing 2-19.

Listing 2-19. Moving Our Object With the Keyboard

```
if(keyboard_check(vk_up) == true) {
        y -= 1;
} else if(keyboard_check(vk_down) == true) {
        y += 1;
}

if(keyboard_check(vk_right) == true) {
        x += 1;
} else if(keyboard_check(vk_left) == true) {
        x -= 1;
}
```

28

In the first line, in our condition for the if statement, we call the function keyboard_check() with the constant vk_down, the virtual key constant for the down arrow on the keyboard. The keyboard_check() function checks if the given key is held down during the Step event and returns a value of either true or false. So, if the up arrow is pressed, then the object is moved one pixel up and when the down arrow is pressed the object is moved one pixel down. Similarly, we move the object one pixel to the right and left when the player holds down the right and left key, respectively. The function returns false when they are not pressed and no action is taken. You will notice that we wrote two separate if statements to handle two sets of keys. If we had combined them together, then only one of them would get executed. Try combining them using an if else and see what happens. Explore the code – (gms2_ch02_03.yyz).

Comparison Operators

GameMaker Studio has a set of comparison operators that come in handy when using the if statement. In the Listing 2-19, we use the short-hand for checking if the value returned by the keyboard_check function is true or not and execute the statements if they are only true. The above can be rewritten in the following way and it will still work:

```
if(keyboard_check(vk_up)) {
        y -= 1;
} else if(keyboard_check(vk_down)) {
        y += 1;
}

if(keyboard_check(vk_right) {
        x += 1;
} else if(keyboard_check(vk_left)) {
        x -= 1;
}
```

Rewriting the movement code using the equality operator.

As you can see, keyboard_check returns either true or false, we use the equality operator represented by two equals to symbols to check if the return value of the function is true or not.

The opposite of the equality operator is the inequality operator or not equal to. This is written by combining two symbols: a not (!) symbol and an equal to (=) symbol. Let's give our small box the ability to move a bit faster when a key is held down and if the key is not held down, we will go with the default speed. Let's add some new variables to store our speed and boost values by adding them into the Create event of the same object (see Listing 2-20).

Listing 2-20. Add Variables for Our Default Speed, Current Speed, and Boost

```
playerSpeed = 1;
playerBoost = 10;
currentSpeed = playerSpeed;
```

Listing 2-21. The Step Event Now Accomodates the Boost

```
if(keyboard_check(vk_shift)) {
        currentSpeed = playerBoost;
} else {
        currentSpeed = playerSpeed;
}

if(keyboard_check(vk_up)) {
        y -= currentSpeed;
} else if(keyboard_check(vk_down) {
        y += currentSpeed;
}
```

```
if(keyboard_check(vk_right)) {
        x += currentSpeed;
} else if(keyboard_check(vk_left)) {
        x -= currentSpeed;
}
```

When the user holds down the shift key, we set the current to our boosted speed value and when the player lets the key go, we set the current speed to our default speed. We also replace the explicit value we used in the movement code with a variable. Run the code to see our little box moving and running when you hold down the shift key. Explore the code in the file gms2_ch02_04.yyz

Now that you understand the difference between the equality (==) and inequality (!=) operators, let's look at some more comparison operators. Let's start by adding a new object into our resources. Create a sprite for the object and fill it with a bright red color. Add the object toward the bottom-center of the room and open the object in the Object Editor. What we are going to do is to automatically move this object across the screen. Think of it as an enemy moving across the screen. Add a Step event to the object and add the code as in Listing 2-22.

Listing 2-22. Moves the Object 10 Pixels to the Right

```
x += 10;
```

If you run the game now, you will see that our new red object moves to the right and disappears off the screen. We want the object to loop back and come through the other side of the screen once it leaves the room. This is shown in Listing 2-23.

Listing 2-23. Pseudocode for What We Are Trying to Achieve

```
If the object's x-position is outside the room toward the
right, then Move the object back to the start of the room.
```

To find out if the object has gone beyond the size of the room, we have two handy variables: room_width and room_height that will provide us with the size of the room. To check if our object has gone outside, all we need to do is to check if the object's x has gone beyond the room_width, since we are moving toward the right. If we were moving toward the left, we would have had to check if our object's x was less than zero. We can rewrite the Step event as shown in Listing 2-24.

Listing 2-24. Loop the Object Back if the Current x-Position of the Object is Greater Than the Room Width

```
x += 10;

if(x > room_width) {
        x = 0;
}
```

Duplicate this object, drag and drop the new object onto the room above the player to the top-middle. Open this object up in the Object Editor and change the Step event so that this new object moves to the left of the screen. As explained earlier, we will have to check if the object has moved to a position outside the screen to the left—that is, if the object's x position is less than zero.

Listing 2-25. Move the Object to the Left and Loop Back to the Right End of the Screen if the Current x-Position of the Object is Less Than Zero

```
x -= 10;

if(x < 0) {
        x = room_width;
}
```

We have changed the code so that the object is moving toward the left of the screen. As the object moves to the left of the screen, its x-value decreases and gets closer to zero, the left end of the room. As the object moves out of the screen we move it by changing the object's x-position the width of the room. The less than or greater than symbol can be substituted with a less than or equal to symbol or greater than or equal to symbol (<= or >=) when the need arises. Explore the code –at yms2_ ch02_06.yyz.

Loops

Loops in GameMaker Studio are just like loops in any other programming language; they are used to repeat a statement or a set of statements a set specific number of times. Each method of looping is slightly different from the others and is used in different situations. Let's explore loops through some examples.

For this section, I've renamed the objects we've created so far to objPlayer, objEnemyRight (the object that keeps moving to the right), and objEnemyLeft (the object that keeps moving to the left). After renaming the object, remove all other instances from the room, apart from the player instance. We will now use create a new object and use it to dynamically add a specific number of new enemy objects randomly into the room.

We start by creating this new empty object, renaming it to objSpawner and adding it to the room. When the game starts, the objSpawner object will create five enemies that move either left or right. Open objSpawner in the Object Editor and add a new Create event. What we will do is to use loops to create a fixed number of enemies that move either left or right on the screen.

Looping With Repeat

The most straightforward way to repeat an action a specific number of times is to use the repeat statement. In the Create event for objSpawner write the code shown in Listing 2-26.

Listing 2-26. Repeat Statement in Action

```
repeat(5) {
        // pick a random x and y position to spawn our enemy
        object
        var dx = irandom_range(0,room_width);
        var dy = irandom_range(0,room_height);

        // pick a random enemy and create an instance of it at
        the random x and y we picked instance_create_layer(dx,dy,
        "Instances", choose(objEnemyRight, objEnemyLeft));
}
```

The repeat statement takes a number as an argument, which designates the number of times the statements within the code block are executed. In Listing 2-26, the code within the curly brackets after repeat(5) gets executed five times. Run the game to see five enemies moving either left or right and the player on the screen.

The irandom_range() functions return a random integer between two given numbers. Here, the first variable dx stores our x-position, a number between zero (our left corner) and the room_width (the right corner). The second variable dy stores our y-position, a number between zero (our top corner) and the room_height (the bottom corner). To make debugging easier, GMS2 uses the same initial random seed. If you want to set your random functions to behave differently every time, you should call the randomize function at the start of your game.

We create an instance of the enemy object at dx and dy. The third parameter of instance_create_layer() is the name of the layer in which instances of objects can be created. A layer called Instances is automatically added to the layers when a room is created. You can add new layers from the properties panel in the Room Editor when you require them. The last parameter is the actual object itself whose instance you want to create. We use the choose function to choose between a set of given values—here, the two objects we want pick from.

Since we will be exploring multiple types of loops to reduce redundancy, we will create a script and move the enemy spawning code there. Add a new script to the Resources Panel, and rename the script to spawnEnemy. Move our enemy spawner code from the loop above to the new script in Listing 2-27 and save it.

Listing 2-27. Enemy Spawner Script

```
/// spawnEnemy - spawn a random enemy at a random position in
your room

// pick a random x and y position to spawn our enemy object
var dx = irandom_range(0,room_width);
var dy = irandom_range(0,room_height);

// pick a random enemy and create an instance of it at the
random x and y we picked
instance_create_layer(dx,dy,"Instances", choose(objEnemyRight,
objEnemyLeft));
```

Now in the Object Editor for objSpawner, we can rewrite the Create event like that in Listing 2-28.

Listing 2-28. Rewriting the Repeat Statement in the Create Event for objSpawner

```
repeat(5) {
        spawnEnemy();
}
```

Our code has now become modular due to the script, and our loop is much shorter and readable. Explore the code in the file gms2_ch02_05.yyz.

Looping With While and Do...Until

The while loop and do...until loops are very similar to each other. Both loop until a specific condition is met. To reiterate our previous example and to understand the similarity or difference, let us look at them side by side (see Listing 2-29).

Listing 2-29. The while Loop and the do...until Loop Side by Side

```
var i = 0;
while(i < 5) {
        spawnEnemy();
        i = i + 1;
}

var i = 0;
do {
        spawnEnemy();
        i = i + 1;
} until(i > 5);
```

In the first case, we declare a variable and set its value to zero, then in the while loop we check if our variable is less than five; if the variable i is less than five then we spawn an enemy. After spawning an enemy, we increment our variable. This will go on for five times, since after each iteration, the while loop checks our condition and deems if it should execute the statements within the braces. Also keep in mind that when we write $(i < 5)$ we imply that the statement $(i < 5)$ == true. Equating to true is assumed and can be omitted to make your code more readable. Explore the code in the file gms2_ch02_06.yyz

In the do...until loop, the difference is very evident. Here, the condition is at the end of the loop and not the beginning, which means that the statements within the loop will get executed at least once before the condition is checked. The second difference is the condition itself, here the loop will continue running until the condition becomes true. Which means the loop will execute until the variable i becomes greater than five. In this case, since the statements inside the loop will execute at least once, we will spawn six instances instead of five. Run the code to see what happens. Explore the code in the file gms2_ch02_07.yyz.

Looping With the for Loop

The for loop is like the while loop, except that it contains the declaration of a variable, a condition if invalidated exits the loop, and a part for incrementing the variable. So, if we were to rewrite the same while loop from our previous example, we can do so like shown in Listing 2-30.

Listing 2-30. The for Loop, Creating Five Enemy Instances

```
for(var i=0; i<5; i++) {
        spawnEnemy();
}
```

If you look at the while loop, you can spot the similarities. The for loop has three distinct parts separated by semi-colons. The first section is for initializing variables. The second part is for a condition that, if false, will cause the loop to end. The third part is used to increment the variable we declared in the first section. Here, in the first section we declare a variable *i* and set it to zero. In the second section, we check if *i* is less than five; if it is less than five, then we spawn an enemy by executing the statements contained within the loop's curly braces. We then increment the variable *i*, which then continue the loop by checking the condition. Run the code to see what happens. Explore the code in the file gms2_ch02_08.yyz

---

OF INFINITE LOOPS

An infinite loop is a loop that does not end; it keeps on running until your game becomes unresponsive and crashes. One needs to be wary of what conditions one lays down before executing code that contains a loop. If your conditions are not as clear as our examples above, or if they depend on results from functions or other arbitrary factors, then one needs to be very careful and should evaluate the code before running it.

The with Construction

We did look at the with construction a while back by changing the color of a bunch of objects. In a way, it works like a loop; it takes an object in your resources and then loops through all the instances of that object in that room. What it does additionally is that the code that is executed is within that object's scope. This is what makes the with construction very special. Let's add some code to the existing example and expand it to see the with construction in action.

In the Step event of our player object, append the code in Listing 2-31.

Listing 2-31. Stopping Traffic With the with Construction

```
with(objEnemyLeft) {
        if(distance_to_object(other)  <= 100) {
                x += 10;
        }
}

with(objEnemyRight) {
        if(distance_to_object(other)  <= 100) {
                x -= 10;
        }
}
```

Both sets of code are like each other, but one set affects the enemy objects moving to the left, and the other set affects the objects moving to the right, separately. In both cases, we use the with construction to loop through each instance of the objects. After switching the scope to an instance, we use the distance_to_object() function to check the distance between this enemy instance's location and the other object— here, referring to the calling object, the player. If the distance between the instance and the player is less than or equal to 100, then we counter the movement. Remember that in the Step event of each enemy object, we are moving the object 10 pixels to the right or left. Here we counter that change by the same value, 10 pixels. So, the overall effect is that the object will remain in its last position. Run the code to see what happens. Explore the code in the file gms2_ch02_09.yyz

The Switch Statement

The switch statement is a set of conditions and set of statements that get executed if a condition is met. It works almost like the *if...else-if... else* statement but suited for longer branching code. It also helps reduce redundancy by clubbing conditions that have the same outcome together. Let's write some code that will give our player sprite some color. We will do so by changing the image_blend variable value to a color, either by setting it to a constant color value or by using a one of the color creation functions. The switch statement structure is as shown in Listing 2-32.

Listing 2-32. Switch Statement Structure

```
switch (expression) {
    case constant:
        // code here
        break;
    default:
        // code here
        break;
}
```

The switch statement takes in an expression that can be evaluated, the result of which is compared to the constant provided with each case statement. The catch here is that the value with which the evaluated result of the expression is compared must be a constant. After each case, we use the break statement to force ourselves out of the switch statement. A default case is provided as a catchall if the expression that is evaluated does not match any of the cases.

We will write our code so that when the player presses the number keys from 1 to 5, the player's sprite will change to a red, green, blue, random color, and original color respectively. Let's use the switch statement to make this work. We will not be using the default case, as we don't want any color change to happen if the user does not press any key.

Listing 2-33. Switch Statements Adding a Tint to the Player (Refer to: gms2_ch02_10.yyz)

```
switch (keyboard_key) {
    case vk_numpad1:
    case 49:
        image_blend = c_red;
        break;
    case vk_numpad2:
    case 50:
        image_blend = c_green;
        break;
    case vk_numpad3:
    case 51:
        image_blend = c_blue;
        break;
    case vk_numpad4:
    case 52:
        image_blend = make_colour_hsv(255, 255, random(255));
        break;
    case vk_numpad5:
    case 53:
        image_blend = c_white;
        break;
}
```

Here, we club two cases, one for the number pad on keyboards as well as the row of number keys on regular smaller laptops. What happens here is that if any of those two cases are true, then the statements below them are executed. To quickly find which keys are mapped to what values, use the show_debug_message() to print the value of keyboard_key.

The break, continue, and exit Statements

There will be cases where you will be required to exit a loop prematurely or to let it skip over to the next step (jump to the increment section or next instance and continue from there).

Listing 2-34. After Spawning Three Enemies, When the Variable i's Value Becomes Two, Exit the Loop

```
for(var i=0; i<5; i++) {
        spawnEnemy();
        if(i == 2) {
                break;
        }
}
```

The break statement works the same way and can be used from within loops, switch statements, and the with statement. In fact, as you have seen before, it is a crucial part of the switch statement.

When the program encounters a continue statement in a loop, it skips the rest of the code and jumps to the start of the next loop. If the continue statement is used outside of a loop, it exits the current scope of execution, which means if the program encounters a continue statement in a script, it exits the script instantly and continues from the calling instance's event. If a continue is encountered in an event, the program exits the event. A continue statement within a with statement causes the script to move the execution to the next instance. The exit statement works in a similar way, but it exits the current script or event and does no further processing.

Listing 2-35. Exits Execution if the Object Is Not Visible

```
if(!visible) exit;
```

In the example in Listing 2-35, if the object's visible property is set to false, it stops from executing any code that comes after it and exits execution.

Now that we have a basic understanding of what GML is and how to write scripts in GameMaker Studio 2 to manipulate your game, the objects within them, as well as how to make your games interactive, we can now move on to making a simple game in the next chapter.

CHAPTER 3

Making Your First Game

Before we create a game within GameMaker Studio (GMS), it is good practice to have your ideas detailed out on paper. I begin almost all my game projects on paper. Designing a game on paper gives you a clear picture of all the rules, systems, mechanics, and the interactions that can happen in a game. Prototyping on paper makes your ideas tangible, playable, easy to test, and changeable early on. Different people have different approaches to Game Design; I practice two different methods that work the best for me. During jams or when you are on a very tight schedule, you would go the tried and tested way of a game mechanics as a first approach. Here, you decide what the player is going to do in the game and then build other layers of information (backstory, the game world, non-playable characters, other interactions, etc.). The second approach that I take is to build out layers of information from a central premise (theme). This approach is slightly more time-consuming and not always successful, but the process brings a lot of clarity, depth, and understanding to the game you are building. For example, you want to build a game around the theme "Heist"; you start by asking questions to yourself about the theme and those involved in it. What is this game about: a heist. Who is stealing and what? From where? And why? Are they alone? If not, how do the others help? Where does the player get his "jobs" from? What motivates the player/avatar? Who are the antagonists? What motivates them?

© Yadu Rajiv 2018
Y. Rajiv, *Developing Turn-Based Multiplayer Games*,
https://doi.org/10.1007/978-1-4842-3861-5_3

The idea here is to build a system of interconnected information sets that eventually lead to a mechanic. In the above example, what is the game about gives you a rough idea of what the player does in the game? When you dig deeper by asking how, you are forced to think in that direction, making choices along the way—one outcome could have been that the player must avoid security systems to steal items from specific locations and escape. Answering one question then leads you to more questions—how does the player avoid security systems? What happens if an alarm is tripped? Do they steal one item or more? How does the player find them in these locations? How will the player escape? These questions bring more clarity to your design and point directly to mechanics, interactions, and features that need to be implemented.

Sketching the Game

For our first small game, we will design and create a Space Shooter. In this game, the player controls a space craft, you shoot at waves of enemies that attack you for points, and you avoid getting shot at by your enemies. The game ends when you die and your high score is saved for eternity, or until the next player beats it. Let's start by sketching out what the game could look like (Figure 3-1).

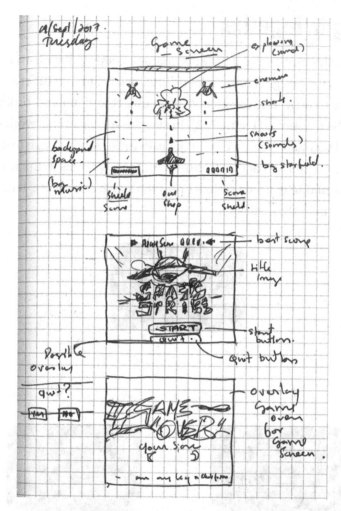

Figure 3-1. *A peek into my notebook; a sketch of the whole game—title screen, game screen, and game over screen, all annotated with quick notes for future reference*

Putting it Together

Now that we have a sketch of how our major screens will look and what components they might contain, let us organize them into different rooms, and then we may be able to organize each object and item accordingly as well in the resources (Figure 3-2). In simpler terms, rooms work like scenes, and you have instances of objects in these rooms. Each instance can listen to events and act accordingly. All the resources in the Resource panel are available to us via scripts or events so we can access, use, and manipulate them dynamically.

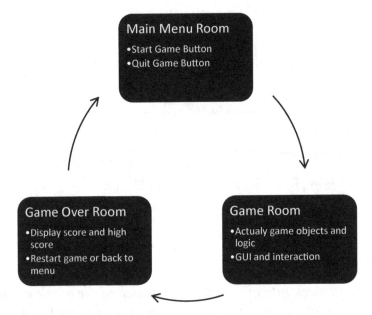

Figure 3-2. *A diagramatic representation of our game and its components*

Starting Our New Project

Let's start by creating a new project using the GameMaker Language and resizing the room to 1024 pixels and 768 pixels for width and height, respectively, like we did in the previous chapter. Once that is done, let's create the background image for the room. In the resources panel on the right side, right-click on sprites and then select Create Sprite. A new sprite called sprite0 is created and you can now see the sprite in your workspace.

The newly opened Sprite Editor can roughly be divided into three parts (Figure 3-3).

- On the left, you have the sprite's name and other properties and functions.

- On the right side toward the top, you see some animation controls and a timeline with one frame in it.

- Toward the bottom, you see a preview of the image contained in that selected frame.

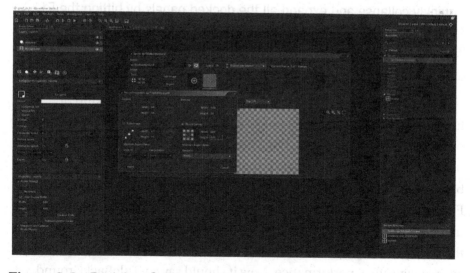

Figure 3-3. *Resizing the new sprite for our title*

For now, we have one frame and it is 64 pixels in width and 64 pixels in height and is empty (transparent). Since we created this sprite to be used as the title background for our game, let's change its size. In the properties to the right you have our sprite's name; let's change that to sprTitleBackGround. It is good practice to name your assets with a prefix (in this case, spr, for sprite) so that you can have unique names for different kinds of assets and can easily differentiate between them.

The second thing we want to do is to change the size of the image. Right below where we changed the Name, the current Size of the image is shown; click the button here with arrows to four corners. In the new window that pops up, select Resize Canvas, and change the size of the image to 640 pixels and 480 pixels for width and height, respectively, and then click apply.

Now to edit our image. With the first frame of our sprite selected, click on the Edit Image button in the Sprite Editor. Clicking this button opens this sprite in the internal image editor.

Tip   At this moment, if you need more space to work with, you can quickly collapse and expand all the docked panels by hitting the F12 key on your keyboard. The same functionality is available as a button on the toolbar as well.

The Image Editor within GMS2 is powerful but lacks the kind of functionality that a dedicated image editing and manipulation program provides. For the time being, I'm using the Image Editor to create a placeholder sprite that we can change later. Now let's add it to the background of the room. Click on the Background layer in the Room Editor, and in the properties, click where it says No Sprite. In the window that pops up, select the sprite that we just created. If you do not need the background to be tiled or stretched, be sure to disable these options, as they may affect performance. Now it should say sprTitleBackGround instead of No Sprite, and you will also notice that the background in the room has also changed (Figure 3-4). Run the game to see it in action.

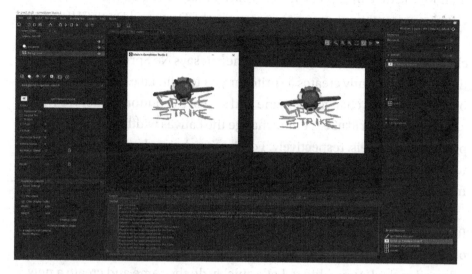

Figure 3-4. *Our game running with a sprite for a background*

Creating Objects and Their Instances

Now that our title screen is partially done, let's add the main two buttons with which the player will interact: the Start button and the Quit button. For that we need to create objects. Objects are GMS's way of storing items that go into the game; so once you create and store an object in your project, you add an instance of that object into a room simply by dragging and dropping it.

Let's create an object now by right-clicking on Objects in the Resources Panel on the right. As soon as you hit Create Object, a new object is created for you and is brought to focus in the workspace. Similarly to the Sprite Editor, the Object Editor shows you the current object's properties. Let's rename this object to objBtnStart—short for object-Button-Start. We will use this as our Start button. You will notice that there is no sprite selected for this object. Without selecting a sprite for an object, that object will not be visible in the game (even when it is marked visible). It is also worth mentioning that an object without a sprite that is marked visible can have visual representations drawn to screen via the Draw and Draw GUI events.

Let's give players something to see and click on; create a new sprite by clicking the plus button right above where it says No Sprite in the Object Editor. This instantly creates a sprite for you to edit. Like we did with the background, let's change the name and size of the button sprite. We will call this sprite sprBtnStart and change the canvas width and height to 128 pixels and 64 pixels, respectively. For the time being, let's just fill the image with a solid color of red and key in start using the text tool available in the Image Editor.

Once you are done editing, close the Image Editor and open the Room. From the Resources Panel drag and drop the newly created objBtnStart into the room (make sure you have the instances layer selected in the Room Editor). Let's quickly do the same and create a new sprite called sprBtnQuit for the Quit button and add it to a new object called objBtnQuit. Once this is done, let's add an instance of this object into the room.

Tip   At times, you will end up having to make many copies of both sprites and objects; to make your life a lot easier, you can duplicate almost everything in the Resources Panel by just right-clicking on the item you want and hitting Duplicate. Although if you see yourself creating too many duplicates, maybe it is a sign that parents, variables, or instance creation code should be used. Having a clear hierarchy will help manage and maintain your projects better as they grow bigger.

For the time being, the buttons that we have created are not functional (Figure 3-5). We want them to behave and function like buttons when interacted with. We can achieve this by working with events.

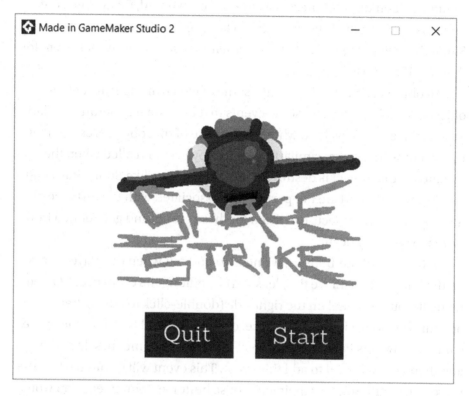

Figure 3-5. *Our non-functional buttons in the running game*

Working With Events

Games, as you know, are perpetually running applications—they are constantly doing something in the background, even if your players are not doing anything. Your game is constantly updating even when there is no user input; it could be updating physics, animating sprites, updating objects and their properties, drawing objects and their sprites to the screen, playing audio, dealing with user input from many devices, and more.

With each update and when new information is processed, GMS2 sends out messages to anyone who wants to listen about these changes and updates. These happenings that GMS2 encounters are called events. For example, when the user presses a key on the keyboard, GMS2 finds out and tells anyone who is listening that a key press event has occurred. Similarly, when the player clicks with their mouse, a mouse click event for that specific mouse button is fired.

All objects can listen for events, some of which are specific to that object and its instance and some events that are global in nature. To clarify, an event like **Create** is fired when an instance of that object is created for the first time in a room; similarly, the Destroy event is called when the instance of that object is destroyed. Whereas, events like Room Start/End and Game Start/End are not particularly associated with the instance of any object, but all objects can listen for these events and get notified by the system when they occur.

In the case of our buttons, we need to find out when the player clicks on the button. To achieve this, let's start by editing the objBtnQuit Object in the Resources Panel on the right side (double-click to edit). After opening the object in the workspace, click on the Add Event button in the connected Events Panel for the object. In the pop-up menu, select Mouse and then Left Released to add this event. This event will get fired when the player clicks and releases their left mouse button on our object. You would have noticed that a new code window has now opened. Let's write some code here.

```
/// @description Handling quit button click

show_debug_message("Quits the game");
```

The first line is a description of what the code does; for us, it handles the click event on the Quit button. The second line prints a message into our Output console. You can see what the code window looks like in Figure 3-6.

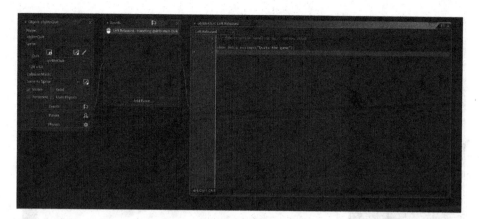

Figure 3-6. *Adding the Left Mouse Released Event to our button*

Tip show_debug_message(...) is a built-in debug function that we will use extensively in the chapters to come. It is a handy way to output data to the console when debugging.

Run the game and click the Quit button to see what happens. You will see Figure 3-7.

55

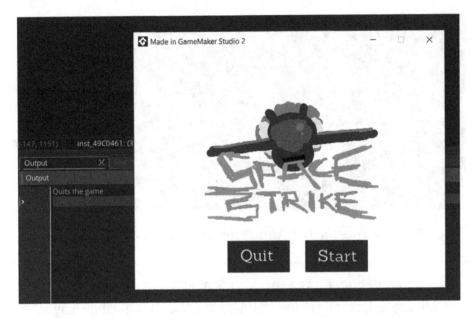

Figure 3-7. *Running the game and clicking the button*

Now that we have the Quit button working, lets implement the code needed to quit the game. To quit a running game, GMS2 has a handy function: game_end(). Calling game_end() destroys all objects and rooms and exits the application. Since some platforms like iOS, Windows UWP, PS4, the Switch, and the browser targets handle how applications are closed, calling the game_end() function can cause an error and your game to crash. Hence, we need to check what platform we are on and then call this function.

What we will do is to add a Create event to both objBtnQuit and objBtnStart and show the appropriate button on the right platform. If the game_end() function can be called, we will let objBtnQuit be, but if it cannot, then we will use the instance_destory function to remove the instance of that button.

Listing 3-1. Code for the Create Event in objBtnQuit

```
if(os_type == os_ios || os_type == os_uwp || os_type ==
os_xboxone || os_type == os_ps4 || os_type == os_switch ||
os_browser != browser_not_a_browser) {
        instance_destroy();
}
```

In the Create event for objBtnStart, if we are to remove the Quit button, then we need to reposition our start button to the center horizontally.

Listing 3-2. Code for the Create Event in objBtnStart

```
if(os_type == os_ios || os_type == os_uwp || os_type ==
os_xboxone || os_type == os_ps4 || os_type == os_switch ||
os_browser != browser_not_a_browser) {
        x = room_width/2 - sprite_width/2;
}
```

The os_type variable holds a value corresponding to the current platform on which the game is running. We check if we are on a valid platform that supports quitting the game and then show only the right button.

Now that we have a working Quit button, let's do the same with our New Game button. The New Game button takes the player to a new session of out space strike game. Before we add any code to the New Game button, we need to create a new room. Let's go ahead and create a new room by right-clicking on the Rooms List in the Resources Panel. In the Resources Panel, right-click on the newly created room and rename it to rmGame.

In the Left Mouse Released event for objBtnStart, we add the code go to our newly created room.

```
room_goto(rmGame);
```

The room_goto() function takes one parameter, which is the number of the room or the name of the room as it appears in the Resources Panel. Run the game to see the Start button in action. Since we have no content in the new room, you will be greeted by an empty black room. In the next section, we look at adding more content and functionality into our game.

To view up to this point in the project, please open the file gms2_ch03_01.yyz.

Creating the Game

Since our goal is learning the interface, we won't dwell too much on making the art but, rather, will import existing artwork. All the assets used in our game can be found in the assets folder along with the projects for Chapter 1.

Our first job is to create our player avatar. Let's do so by creating a sprite and importing our player ship into GamerMaker Studio. To create a new sprite, you need to right-click on the sprites section in the Resources Panel, and then click on *Create Sprite*. Once the sprite has been created, it will come into focus in our workspace. Click the Import button on the Sprite Editor to import our player's avatar spacecraft. Finally, rename the sprite to sprPlayer.

Once the right image has been imported into the sprite, we move on to create an object for the player's ship. Create a new object and rename it to objPlayer and assign our newly created sprite for it (sprPlayer).

Once you are done, drag and drop the objPlayer object onto our empty room: rmGame (see Figure 3-8).

Figure 3-8. The player's ship in the new room

Our next step is to make the player ship move according to the player's input. For this game, we will only be using the mouse for both movement and firing bullets. We will also restrict the player's movement to the horizontal (x) axis.

Add a new Step event to our player's object: `objPlayer`. Once this is done, update the player's x-position to that of the current mouse x-position.

```
x = mouse_x;
```

Run the game now and you will see that as you move the mouse, the ship also moves along the x-axis. Now that we have the ship moving, let's add some firepower!

Firing Bullets

Firing and bullets are two different problems that we need to solve. Firing involves processing input from the player, firing (creating an instance of) a bullet and then waiting a fixed amount of time before firing again, if required. Bullets themselves are objects that, once created, will travel in a direction with a set speed. When they hit enemy players, they affect the enemy in some way and get destroyed.

To fire a bullet, we first need to create one. Like with the player object, we start by creating a sprite for the bullet. Once the sprite is created, create a new object and add our sprite it. Once done, rename the object to objLaserBlue. Once the object has been created add a Create event for it. Add the following code in the Create event for the laser:

```
vspeed = -20;
```

Objects have a bunch of very useful properties that we can take advantage of—one of them being the vertical speed of that object. Once the vertical speed of that object has been set, it will start and continue to move vertically with each frame. Since we want this bullet to go upward, we have set its vertical speed to -20. Now that the bullet has been created, it is a matter of firing it.

Our bullets need to be fired when the player clicks the mouse left button and when the mouse button is held down. If the mouse button is held down, it needs to fire at a fixed interval. To achieve this, let's add two events: one for Create and the next for Global Left Down.

In the Create event for the player object, we create a new variable that is used to count the number of frames that have passed since a bullet was fired.

```
shotCounter = 0;
```

In then Mouse, Global, Left Down event for objPlayer, add the following code:

```
/// @description player firing

if((shotCounter % 10) == 0) {
        shotCounter = 0;
        instance_create_layer(x-12, y-12, "Instances",
        objLaserBlue);
        instance_create_layer(x+8, y-12, "Instances",
        objLaserBlue);
}

shotCounter++;
```

The Step events of all objects in the room get called on each frame. Our frame rate or the number of times the room is updated and drawn is fixed and is set in the Options/Main dialog in the Resources Panel (unlike the old GMS, where the fps was set per room). Our game is currently drawn at a rate of 30 frames per second (Figure 3-9). This means our Step event gets called 30 times every second. We use the `instance_create_layer()` function to create an instance of objLaserBlue at the player's current position, every 10 frames.

Figure 3-9. *Main game options dialog, where our frame rate is currently set to 30 fps*

There are two functions that let you create an instance of an object in a room and they are:

```
instance_create_depth(x, y, depth, obj);
```

and

```
instance_create_layer(x, y, layer_id, obj);
```

When using instance_create_depth(), it takes an x- and y-parameter, which determine where the new instance of the object (obj) should be placed, and a depth at which the object should be created. Since all instances of objects must be created inside a layer, GMS creates and manages a layer if you use this function. This is an internally managed layer, and you have no access to this. We use the second function to explicitly create our laser instances in our primary Instances layer. The layer_id is the name of the layer we want this instance to be created in, passed in as a string. So, when the user clicks anywhere on the screen using the left mouse button, we create two instances of our objLaserBlue object at either side of the player where our two cannons are located. Once these instances are created, because of the vspeed we have set, they move upward with each passing frame.

Adding Sound to Your Shots

To make this a bit juicier, let's add a bullet firing sound to the mix. Before we can play a sound, we need to add it to our resources. To add a sound, right-click on the Sounds Section in the Resources Panel and select Create Sound. In the new panel that opens in the workspace, change the name of the sound to sndLaser_fire_2 (Figure 3-10).

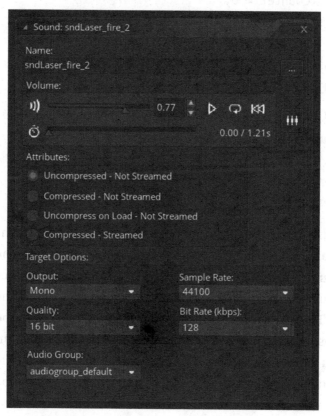

Figure 3-10. *Creating a sound resource, loading an audio file, and previewing it*

Click the button with three dots next to where you edited the name to load the actual sound files from your assets folder. Open and load the file named sfx_laser2.ogg. Click the Play button in the controls to hear a preview of the sound. Once we have our sound loaded, let's add to our firing code in objPlayer's Global Left Mouse event. Since we only want to play the sound when we fire the laser, we will add it inside our already existing if condition and our new code will look like

```
/// @description player firing

if((shotCounter % 10) == 0) {
        shotCounter = 0;
        instance_create_layer(x-12, y-12, "Instances",
        objLaserBlue);
        instance_create_layer(x+8, y-12, "Instances",
        objLaserBlue);

        // play laser firing sounds
        audio_play_sound(sndLaser_fire_2, 10, false);

}

shotCounter++;
```

The audio_play_sound() function takes three parameters, the index or name of the sound resource(it is worth noting that the name is the actual resource name in the Resources Panel and not a string), a number that lets the audio subsystem know how important playing back this sound is, and a Boolean (True or False) value stating if this sound must be looped or not. Different systems can play a different number of sounds simultaneously, and this is a limited number. The value you pass to this function as the priority dictates which sounds are played and which sounds stop playing when the channel limit has been reached. In our case, this won't be a problem, as we are not playing too many sounds simultaneously.

```
audio_play_sound(index, priority, loop);
```

Now that we can fire lasers, let's do a bit of housekeeping. All these lasers we have created are slowly moving outward due to their vspeed, and they will not stop until the game ends. Each laser takes up a small chunk of memory and processing power of both the CPU and the GPU; it may not be much, but when you fire of hundreds and thousands of them, they all add up to a huge number. So, to save ourselves from this memory bottleneck we must destroy these lasers once they are of no use to us. In our case, once the laser is beyond the scope of the room, we can safely say that they are of no use to us. GMS has a handy way of telling instances when they are outside of the room. GMS does it by calling the Outside Room event. To add this event, open up the objLaserBlue object and add the Event from Other/Outside Room. Once we are outside the room, we tell GMS to destroy that instance by calling the instance_destroy() function.

```
/// @description Clean up when outside the room

instance_destroy();
```

The instance_destroy() function takes two optional parameters: the first one is the id to the object to be destroyed, which by default is the calling instance, and the second optional argument is a Boolean value if the Destroy event for the object should be called, which by default is true. Apart from the calling object, you can pass in an id of an object you want to destroy. You can also destroy all instances of an object by passing in the object's name from the Resources Panel. You can further use the special keywords other or all with this function as well.

```
instance_destroy([id, execute_event_flag]);
```

Hiding the Cursor

Before we move on to creating enemies we can shoot at, let's do a bit of cleaning up. Right now, when you move the mouse cursor around, you can see that your ship follows it in the x-axis. The problem is your mouse cursor can be a distraction. Let's hide the mouse cursor when we are playing the game.

Like the Create event in objects, the room also has a Create event. This event is called once when each room is created. As good practice and for ease of management, we will create a script resource and then call this script resource from our Room's Create event.

To create a script resource, right-click on the scripts section in the Resources Panel and select Create Script. The newly created script opens in your workspace; let's rename it to something memorable. Since this is code that gets executed once when rmGame is created, let's rename to scrGameCreate. In our script, let's write the code to hide our mouse.

```
/* hide the mouse */
window_set_cursor(cr_none);
```

window_set_cursor() takes in one parameter, which is what cursor to use. We pass in a system constant, cr_none, which tells GMS that we are not using a cursor. Now that we have the code in place, let's execute this script when the room gets created.

To access a room's Create event, you must open a room in the Room Editor. In the Resources Panel, under Rooms, double-click to open rmGame in the Room Editor. In the Room Editor's properties panel, on the left toward the bottom, you can find that room's properties (Figure 3-11).

Figure 3-11. *Click the Creation Code button to see the code that gets executed when this room is created*

Click the button labeled Creation Code, and this will open the room's Create event. Any script you write here will be executed once when the room is created. From here we are going to execute the Script Resource we have created.

```
scrGameCreate();
```

We will call `scrGameCreate()` just like any other function from within the room's Create event.

Now when we run the game and click on the Start button, the mouse cursor is hidden from us in the new room. At the onset, it might seem a bit too much to do these two extra steps, but in the longer run having all your scripts in one place makes for easy editing and management.

Going to Space

We have a ship on the screen; we can move it around and shoot some lasers. To make it a bit more like we are in space, let's add some backgrounds. Just like we created the background for the main menu, we will first create a sprite with the images we want to use as our background for our game. The only difference is that instead of selecting just one image, we will use four images. Load the four background images from the assets folder UI/bg into a sprite, and rename it to sprBg (Figure 3-12). In the Sprite Editor, make sure that you have set the animation speed to 0, so that these sets of backgrounds are not animated.

Figure 3-12. *Setting our newly created sprite as the background for the room*

Open rmGame and select the background layer-I have renamed mine to backgroud_space. As we did before, click on the button labeled No Sprite and select our newly created sprBg as the sprite to use. Since our background image is smaller than the room size, let's set it so that the image can be tiled vertically and horizontally. To do this, check the two check boxes labeled Horizontal Tile and Vertical Tile. Now that we have them tiled, let's animate them! GMS lets you set a horizontal and vertical speed for its background layers. Let's change Vertical Speed to 5 so that the background moves from top to bottom. Run the game now and you will see that we are now flying through space. Feel free to play around with the horizontal and vertical speed components to see what happens.

To make things a bit more interesting, let's change the background space image every time you start the game to a random one. Our sprBg sprite already contains four subimages—all we need to do is to change the background image of the layer to a random one every time the room starts. To do this we will add some code to the Create event of the room. Earlier in the chapter we created a script resource to be executed when rmGame is created; we can reuse the same script and append changes to it to set our random space background.

```
/// @description this script is executed when rmGame is created

/* hide the mouse */
window_set_cursor(cr_none);

/* set a random image from our background sprite as our
backround for this room */
var lay_id = layer_get_id("Background_space");
var back_id = layer_background_get_id(lay_id);
var bg_index = irandom(3);
layer_background_index(back_id, bg_index);
```

Right below where we hid the mouse cursor, we use the layer_get_id() function to get the id for our background layer, here called Background_space. Once we have the id for the layer, we use that id to get the id associated with the background for the layer. We can then use one of the many layer_background_* functions to manipulate the background. Here we need to randomly change the index of the background. Our sprite contains four frames, and these subimages are indexed from 0 to 3, which makes four images. By default, the first image in the sprite is used. We use the irandom() function to generate a number between 0 and 3 (inclusive) and then use the layer_background_index() function to set the index of the background. Now, every time you start the game, it will have a different background.

Upgrading the Main Menu

Before we wrap up and move to tackling Enemies, let's change our placeholder background and buttons in the main menu. To change the background for the main menu, open the sprTitleBackGround sprite in the Sprite Editor. In the Sprite Editor, click on the import button and select our new background from the assets folder: UI/bgMenu.png. Once the background is changed, similarly import two button sprites from the for each button. The Start button has two states represented by two images in the assets folder: btnStart.png and btnStart_over.png. When you import the images into the existing sprBtnStart sprite, be sure to select both the images. Once both the images are imported into the sprite, be sure to set its animation speed to 0. Similarly import the two images, btnQuit.png and btnQuit_over.png, for the sprBtnQuit sprite. Once the button sprites are in place, let's add a small bit of code to make use of the new images we have added.

Figure 3-13. Our new main menu and buttons on the left. The player on a random space bg moving and shooting. To view up to this point in the project, please open the file gms2_ch03_02.yyz.

In objBtnStart add two more events: Mouse enter and Mouse leave. Add the following code to each of them, respectively.

```
/// @description Button hover
image_index = 1;
```

and on the Mouse leave event

```
/// @description Button Hover leave
image_index = 0;
```

What this essentially does is when the player moves the mouse cursor over an instance of the button object, we swap the current subimage with the second one (here with the index 0). When the mouse leaves, then we swap back to the initial frame of the image. Repeat the same with objBtnQuit, and we are good to go.

To view up to this point in the project, please open the file gms2_ch03_02.yyz.

Handling Enemies

Now that we can shoot, let's add some targets to shoot at. What we will do in this section is to add enemy sprites and objects, make our lasers collide with them, destroy the enemy sprites and replace them with an explosion, add sounds for those explosions, update the player's score for destroying each enemy, and finally have a mechanism in place to spawn multiple enemies automatically.

Let's jump right in and create a new sprite from the Resources Panel; once the sprite is created rename it to sprEnemy01 and use the Import button to import an image from the assets folder—enemies/spaceShips_003.png. Once the image is in place, add a new object to our resources. Once the object is created, rename it to objEnemy01 and associate our sprite to the object.

Just like we did with our lasers, to make our enemy move toward us and once the enemy moves outside of the room, we need to destroy it. Start by adding a Create event to the enemy object. In the Create event, we will set the vspeed variable so that the object moves down toward us.

```
/// @description Initialized
// set out vertical speed, moves the object from top to bottom
vspeed = 6;

// value of this ship - points given for shooting it down
shipPoints = 10;

// activate alarm number 0 after room_speed * 5 = 5 seconds in
frames
alarm[0] = room_speed * 5;
```

Apart from the vertical speed, we will also create an instance variable called shipPoints and set it to 10. Instance variables are variables that are accessible within the scope of an instance, which means that variable, once set, can be accessed and updated from any event within the object.

Since we want the ships to start coming into the screen from outside of the room, we can't use the Outside room event for housekeeping like we did with the laser beams. So, in the third statement, we set an alarm for 5 seconds. An alarm is exactly that—it is a timer that is unique to an object; when a set amount of time expires, an event is fired. Each object can have up to 11 alarms and when setting an alarm, one should also create a corresponding Alarm[0...11] event as well. GMS alarms use frames instead of seconds; what this means is that when one wants an alarm to go off after 1 second, the value that you set the alarm to is the number of frames in 1 second. In our case, we use the built-in variable called room_speed (which is by default set to 30 frames per second), which equals the number of frames in a second, and multiply it by five to get the number of frames in 5 seconds. So eventually when 5 seconds elapse, the Alarm 0 event for the object gets called, and the following code is executed, destroying our enemy space ship.

```
/// @description destory this object
instance_destroy();
```

Now that the enemy is ready, let' create a new layer for it in the room. Create a new instance layer called Enemies in rmGame via the Room Editor. Add our enemy object to this layer by dragging and dropping it into the room. Run the game to see the enemy flying toward you.

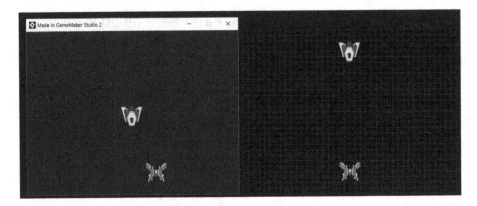

Figure 3-14. *The enemy flying toward the bottom of the screen on the left and the enemy in the room on the right*

Shooting the Enemy

We now have an enemy on the screen and we can shoot lasers. Putting them together, we now must add functionality to the enemy so that it can handle collisions with our lasers. Whenever the enemy collides with the laser we have fired, it should destroy itself, destroy the laser object that it was hit with, update the score, play a sound, and then play an explosion animation.

First, let's add a way to save our score. Let's create a global variable to hold our player's score for each level. A global variable is a variable that is accessible across rooms and instances. We are creating a global variable since we will need access to the score even after the game ends. Since the score is something that is reset at the beginning of each level, let's add a global variable to rmGame's create event. Let's open our script resource scrGameCreate and add a global variable here, as it is called every time rmGame starts.

```
/// @description this script is executed when rmGame is created

/* hide the mouse */
window_set_cursor(cr_none);

/* set a random image from our background sprite as our
backround for this room */
var lay_id = layer_get_id("Background_space");
var back_id = layer_background_get_id(lay_id);
var bg_index = irandom (3);
layer_background_index(back_id, bg_index);

/* our score */
global.playerScore = 0;
```

We will append our `playerScore` variable to the end of the script. To create a variable in the global scope, you use the word global followed by the dot operator and then a variable name you would want to use—in our case, `playerScore`. Initially, when the room starts, we set the `playerScore` global variable to 0. Every time an enemy gets hit with our lasers, we will add the enemy's value to our score.

GameMaker provides an easy way to check for collisions between objects. Open the `objEnemy01` object in the Object Editor; in events, add a new Collision event and select `objLaserBlue` from the dropdown list (Add Event/Collision/objLaserBlue). This event gets called every time there is a collision between `objLaserBlue` and `objEnemy01` instances.

```
/// @description Getting shot
global.playerScore += shipPoints;

instance_destroy(other);
instance_destroy();
```

In the first statement, we increment the global variable `global.playerScore` with the points we get for shooting this ship. In the second and third statements, we destroy our ship along with the other object that collided with us—in this case, the built-in variable `other` contains the laser that hit the enemy ship.

Run the game and shoot the enemy to see both your bullet and the enemy disappear. This looks pretty good, but we should juice it up with some audio and an explosion animation. Let's load a sound file for our explosion and create a new sprite for our animation. The sound folder inside assets contains a file called `snd_boom_0.wav`. Create a new sound resource and load this sound into it; once the sound is loaded, rename the newly created sound resource to `sndEnemyHit`. Create a new sprite for our explosion animation, rename this to `sprBoom,` and import all the images inside the effects folder in assets. Once the import is complete, set the speed of the animation to 30 frames per second. Create a new object resource called `objBoom` for our explosion object and add `sprBoom` as its sprite.

Now that we have our resources in place, we need to make sure that the audio is played when the explosion happens, and then the explosion should remove itself from the room once it has played through the animation one complete time. We will play the audio in the Create Event for the `sprBoom` object so that the explosion sound gets played when `sprBoom` is first added into the room.

```
/// @description Create the boom object with audio
audio_play_sound(sndEnemyHit,1,false);
```

Now, we need to find out if our animation has played through at least once. To do this we will use the built-in instance variables, `image_index`, and `image_number`. The `image_index` variable returns the current index of the subimage that is being displayed. When our animation is played back, GMS cycles through the subimages for the current instance of the sprite at a rate of a given frames per second or frames per game frame, which is set in the Sprite Editor. This rate can further be controlled using the image_speed instance variable, which acts like a multiplier. By default, the image_speed is 1; changing it to 0.5 will half the animation speed, and changing it to 1.5 will double it. GMS changes the image_index variable to the appropriate number internally as it cycles through each of these subimages. The image_number variable is a read-only variable that returns the number of subimages the sprite contains. Keep in mind that the image_index is 0-based and image_number is 1-based, which means if you have one subimage, image_index for the sprite will be 0, whereas the image_number for the sprite will be 1. Armed with this information, we can find out exactly when the animation has finished playing in an instance of objBoom and remove it like shown here:

```
/// @description remove once done playing
if(image_index >= image_number - 1) {
        instance_destroy();
}
```

Each time the Step event is called, we check to see if the current image_index is greater than or equal to the last image index (computed by subtracting 1 from the total number of subimages—the image_number). If we have displayed the last frame of the sprite, then we destroy the sprite. The other much simpler way to do the same would be to add an Animation End event in the objBoom Object. The Animation End event (located in Other events) is triggered when the animation for the sprite attached to the object comes to an end. You can use the instance_destory() function from within the Animation End event to achieve the same results. Add an Animation End vent to objBoom and add the following lines of code there:

```
/// @description remove once done playing
instance_destroy();
```

Now that we have an explosion with sound ready, let's add it to the collision code in our enemy object.

```
/// @description Getting shot
global.playerScore += shipPoints;

var boom = instance_create_layer(x, y,"Enemies", objBoom);
boom.vspeed = vspeed;

instance_destroy(other);
instance_destroy();
```

When the enemy is hit by our laser, we use the instance_create_layer() function to add the objBoom object at the current x- and y-position of the enemy ship. We go a bit beyond this as well. If we examine the instance_create_layer() or instance_create_depth() function, we can see that the function returns the id of the newly created object. This means that as soon as you create an object, you have access to it to do what you please.

When a new instance of objBoom is created we save its id to a local variable called boom. Through boom, we change the vertical speed of the newly created explosion animation. We do this to avoid a small visual discrepancy; since we are simulating moving forward and the enemy is moving backward, a sudden static animation on the screen stands out from the rest. To avoid this, we set the explosions vspeed.

Spawning Enemies

We have one enemy on the screen right now. It would be tempting to keep placing more and more enemies in the room, but at some point, it becomes a difficult exercise—the amount of variation that you can create reduces drastically after placing a small number on screen. To avoid this, we will create a factory that produces enemies constantly at a set interval.

Let's start by creating an object from the Resource Panel and renaming it to objEnemySpawner. In the Object Editor, be sure to uncheck the box for visible. This will make sure that our spawner object itself will not be visible. You can go ahead and choose or make a sprite if you want so that you have a visual cue in the Game Editor. It is a good practice to have custom sprites for your invisible objects, as it becomes easier to find them in rooms and edit them. By default, an object without a sprite is represented by a question mark symbol inside a grey circle.

Once you have your spawner object made, add it to our rmGame room. Double-click on the instance, and in the Instance Editor, click Edit Object. We want our spawner to produce enemy ships at a constant interval; the last time we needed a way to destroy enemy ships after an interval, we used an alarm; let's do the same here. We will set up an alarm so that when the alarm interval is up, an enemy ship is created at a random location right outside the top part of the room.

```
/// @description Enemy Spawnner Initiated

// speed at which enemies should be spawning
spawnSpeed = room_speed * 1.5;

alarm[0] = spawnSpeed;
```

In the Create event of the objEnemySpawner object, we set an alarm to go off one and a half times the room_speed—that would mean every 1.5 seconds.

```
/// @description Alarm spwans enemys when called

var ex = irandom_range(50, room_width - 50);
var ey = -100;
instance_create_layer(ex, ey,"Enemies",objEnemy01);
alarm[0] = spawnSpeed;
```

In the Alarm 0 event, we pick a random point between 50 and room_
width—50 is for our enemy's x-position, and the y-position is 100 pixels
outside and above the room. We then use the instance_create_layer()
function to create an objEnemy01 object at this location. In the last line, we
reset the alarm to go off in another 1.5 seconds.

Figure 3-15. *Setting up the spawner*

Run the game to shoot some enemies and to see them spawn every 1.5
seconds.

Displaying Our Score

Every time we shoot an enemy, our `global.playerScore` global variable gets updated. All that is left to do is to show it to the player. To do this we will create an object and, using its draw event, draw the score onto the screen. Before we go ahead, install the two fonts provided in the assets UI/fonts folder. We will use one of these fonts to draw the text on the screen. But before we can use these fonts, make sure you install them on your computer. On Windows or a Mac, you can open the font file by double-clicking on them and clicking the Install button that is displayed in the window that opens.

To use the font we have installed, we need to create a font resource. Right-click on the Fonts section in the Resources Panel and select Create Font. In the Font Editor that opens in the workspace, rename the font to fntHUD. Then from the dropdown below, select one of the fonts we just installed-KenVector Future Thin. Change the size of the font to 14, and we are done. Now that the font resource is in place, let's draw some text.

To show our score, let's create a new object in the Objects section. Let's rename it to objScore. Since we will be doing the drawing, we don't need a sprite. Double-click the objScore object to open it in the Object Editor. Add a new Draw GUI event to the object. The Draw GUI event is a special event that is called every frame and is used to draw user interface elements. Unlike the Draw event, Draw GUI draws elements are special events that are designed for drawing GUI elements. They are unaffected by position, rotation. or scale of the cameras and viewports in a room. It is important to understand that even with views enabled, the draw coordinates do not change and (0,0) will always remain at the top

left-hand corner of the application surface or the display. For more
nuances of Draw events, please do check the related documentation:
`https://docs2.yoyogames.com/source/_build/2_interface/1_editors/`
`events/draw_events.html`

```
/// @description Displaying the score
```

```
// set the font and alignment
draw_set_font(fntHUD);
draw_set_valign(fa_middle);
draw_set_halign(fa_left);
```

```
// draw the text
draw_text(x, y, "SCORE: " + string(global.playerScore));
```

Before we draw the score, we use the formatting functions to set the
font to fntHUD. We then set the vertical and horizontal alignment of the
text, and finally we draw the text at the x- and y-location of our object itself.
This means the text will be drawn where we place this object. The final
parameter in draw_text() is the actual string to be drawn.

We add together the text "SCORE: " with the playerScore; we use the
string function to convert the playerScore from a number to a string.
Without this conversion, when you try to add a string with a number, GMS
will throw an error. Place objScore close to the bottom left of the screen
and run the game to see our score text in action. To view up to this point in
the project, please open the file gms2_ch03_03.yyz.

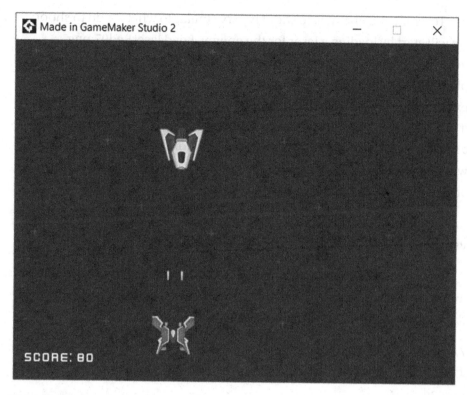

Figure 3-16. Shooting and scoring

Our Enemies Fight Back

In this section we will see the enemy fighting back, giving us a taste of their red lasers. We will also deal collision detection for both the lasers and the enemy ships. If we get hit with their lasers or bump into an enemy ship, we explode and it is game over. Our ship will explode like the enemy ships, and once that is done, we'll move to the next room showing us a game over screen as well as our score. If our score is the same as or more than the high score for the session, then we tell the player that we have a high score and save it too.

Teaching the enemies to shoot is very similar to what we do to shoot; we will start by loading a laser for the enemy. Load laserRed07.png from assets/laser and create a sprite called sprLaserRed. Since both our player and enemy lasers are almost identical, we can just duplicate the existing blue laser, so go ahead and duplicate objLaserBlue and rename it objLaserRed. The only change we must make will be the vspeed; since objLaserRed must travel down toward the bottom of the screen, its vspeed will now need to change to a positive number. Open the Step event for objLaserRed and change the vspeed to 20.

```
/// @description The laser shot
vspeed = 20;
```

Now, we will set up an alarm and an Alarm event to handle that alarm in the objEnemy01 object. Since we already have an alarm, we will now use the next available alarm, which is Alarm 1.

```
/// @description Initialized
// set out vertical speed, moves the object from top to bottom
vspeed = 6;

// activate alarm number 0 after room_speed * 5 = 5 seconds in frames
alarm[0] = room_speed * 5;

// value of this ship - points given for shooting it down
shipPoints = 10;

// speed at with the enemy fires
fireSpeed = room_speed * random_range(0.2,2);

// every fireSpeed frames, do this!
alarm[1] = fireSpeed;
```

The fireSpeed variable stores how fast our alarm should go off, and we choose a random a time between 0.2 seconds and 5 seconds, which means that some enemies might shoot at us fast (every 0.2 seconds), while some fire late (after 2 seconds).

```
/// @description When this alarm goes off fire!

instance_create_layer(x, y, "Enemies", objLaserRed);

// play laser firing sounds
audio_play_sound(sndLaser_fire_1, 10, false);

alarm[1] = fireSpeed;
```

In the Alarm 1 event, we create an instance of the objLaserRed object at the enemy ship's x- and y-location using instance_create_layer(). We play the same laser firing sound we used for the player and then reset the alarm to fireSpeed. Run the game to see how your enemies now fight back.

They can shoot all they want, but you would have noticed that none of those lasers are hitting us. Let's add a Collision event to the player object, objPlayer. Add a collision event to objPlayer with the objLaserRed object.

```
/// @description We got shot!

var boom = instance_create_layer(x, y,"Instances", objBoom);
boom.vspeed = vspeed;

//destroy the laser
instance_destroy(other);

// destroy our ship
instance_destroy();
```

Just like we did with the enemy object when it collided with our blue laser, we create an instance of the boom object, which has the explosion

sound and animation. Then we destroy the laser we got shot with using
`instance_destroy()` and passing the other (in this case the `objLaserRed`
object). And then we destroy the ship itself.

If you run the game now, you will see that you are getting shot and
destroyed, but the game keeps on going. Once your ship is destroyed, after
the explosion is done, we need to take the user to a game over screen and
present our score. To do this, let's make a new room.

Create a new room and call it `rmGameOver`. Create a new sprite in the
Resources Panel and load up the background image (`bgGameOver.png`) that
we are going to use in this room from assets/UI folder. Once the image is
loaded, set the sprite as the background for the room. If our newly created
room is bigger than the other rooms, change the width and height of the
room to 640 and 480 pixels, respectively, in the Properties Panel on the left
in the Room Editor.

Now that we have a game over screen, let's tell GMS to show it once
our ship is destroyed. How can we achieve this? We want the game over
screen to show up once our ship is destroyed and the explosion is done
playing. We are using `objBoom` for the sound and explosion animation for
both the player and enemy ships. If we make any changes to `objBoom`, they
will affect not just us but also the enemies as well. Since we don't want
the game over screen to be shown when we shoot down enemies, let's
duplicate the `objBoom` and make a new object specially for the player.

Go to the `rmGame` room and duplicate `objBoom`; rename it
`objBoomPlayer` and open it in the Object Editor. In the Animation End
event, make these changes.

```
/// @description remove once done playing

instance_destroy();
window_set_cursor(cr_arrow);
room_goto(rmGameOver);
```

In the Step event, we check if the animation has finished playing, and once it is done, we remove the instance of the explosion from the room using the `instance_destroy()` function. Once the instance is removed, we set our cursor to an arrow and then use the `room_goto()` function to go to the `rmGameOver` room.

Now that we have our new `objBoomPlayer` object, in our Collision event with the red laser, we need to create a new instance of `objBoomPlayer` instead of `objBoom`; let's do that now.

```
/// @description We got shot!

var boom = instance_create_layer(x, y,"Instances",
objBoomPlayer);
boom.vspeed = vspeed;

//destroy the laser
instance_destroy(other);

// destroy our ship
instance_destroy()
```

Everything else remains the same, except for the last parameter passed to the `instance_create` function. Instead of `objBoom`, we pass in the newly created `objBoomPlayer` object. Run the game and see what happens when you get shot. You will see that once we get shot, the sound and the explosion animation are played and our new game over room is shown.

The second way that the game can get over is by us colliding with the enemy ships; if we hit any enemy ship, both ships are destroyed and the game over screen is shown. Most of the collision code remains the same, except we need to now destroy the enemy ship and add an animation for that as well. Create a new Collision event for `objPlayer` with `objEnemy01`.

```
/// @description collision with the enemy

// create an explosion object for our player
var boom = instance_create_layer(x, y,"Instances",
objBoomPlayer);
boom.vspeed = vspeed;

// create an explosion object for our enemy (other) and destroy it
with(other) {
        var boom = instance_create_layer(x, y,"Enemies", objBoom);
        boom.vspeed = vspeed;
        instance_destroy();
}

// destroy our ship
instance_destroy()
```

The code is very similar to our collision code with the laser, the only difference here is that instead of just destroying the other object with the instance_destroy() function, we add an extra step of creating an instance of the objBoom for the enemy ship. We do that using the with statement. As seen in the last chapter, the with statement is a special statement used to switch the scope of the code executed within its braces to be in the scope of the object passed to it. Here we switch the scope from the player object's instance to the other instance (being an instance of objEnemy01). Once in the other instance's scope, we create a new instance of objBoom at the x- and y-coordinates of the enemy. We also set the objBoom instance's vspeed to the enemy ships vspeed. Once this is done, we destroy the enemy instance by calling the instance_destroy() function from within the scope of the with statement.

Our game over screen is functional; it tells people that the game is over. But, it would be better if we show what their score is, if they beat their high scores, and a way to get back to the main menu where they can either choose to play again or exit the game.

Let's try to get that score and high score message on the screen. To do this, we need a way to store our high score. At the start of the session the high score is reset to 0. But with each session, the high score is set to the highest score the player has achieved. We need to declare a global variable to store this high score value.

Our first impulse is to add a global variable in the menu, but let's create a new room to store and initialize all global variables that we need to create and initialize once across the game. This gives you access to one point where all initialization for the game can happen, and this will not change even if a menu might. Let's add a new room called rmInit in the Rooms section in the Resources Panel. Once this is done, drag the newly created rmRoom item to the top of the list so that rmInit is the first room in the Rooms section. The first room in the Rooms section is the first room to be run by GMS. Let's resize the room and add a script for the Create event for this room.

First add a new script in the Scripts section of the Resources Panel and rename it to scrInitCreate. Then, open the rmInit room in the Room Editor and in the Properties Panel, change the width and the height of the room to 640 and 480 pixels, respectively. In the properties panel, click on the checkbox labeled Persistent. Making a room persistent is a way of telling GMS that it shouldn't destroy the room once we leave it. All rooms and objects that are not persistent are destroyed when the player switches a room. Once this is done, open the Creation Code for the room.

```
scrInitCreate();
```

In the Creation Code, call our scrInitScript script, which for the time being is empty. Let's open the scrInitCreate Script to initialize our new high score global variable.

```
global.highScore = 0;
```

```
room_goto(rmMenu);
```

In the first line, we add the global variable called global.highScore and set its value to 0. In the second line, we tell GMS to go to the rmMenu room.

Tip   To quickly open rooms, scripts, sprites, or objects from code, click on the item's name with the middle mouse button (wheel button) or select the item and then hit the F1 key.

Now that we have the highScore global variable, what we will do is to duplicate the objScore object and rename it to objGameOverMessage. Add it to the Instances layer of the rmGameOver room. Place it in the middle of the room. The objScore object we duplicated was used to display the score; let's edit it to show the score as well as a message if we have the high score.

```
/// @description Displaying the score

// set the font and alignment
draw_set_font(fntHUD);
draw_set_valign(fa_middle);
draw_set_halign(fa_center);

// draw the text
if(global.playerScore >= global.highScore) {
        global.highScore = global.playerScore;
        draw_text(x, y, "Your Score is " + string(global.
        playerScore) + "\nYou have the new High Score!");
} else {
        draw_text(x, y, "Your Score is " + string(global.
        playerScore));
}
```

Since we are keeping the object in the middle of the screen, we will change the horizontal alignment to `fa_center` from `fa_left`. We then check if the player's current score is higher than or equal to the high score for this session. If the player's score is higher, then we set our high score to the player's current score and show a message whicthath tells the player that they have the new high score. If not, we just display the player's current score.

To take us back to the main menu, let's add a button. Let's duplicate and existing button so that we can reuse all the events for the button. Once you duplicate a button, rename it to `objBtnMenu`. Open the object in the Object editor. Near the preview of the sprite, click on the *New Sprite* button. Once the Sprite Editor opens, rename the new sprite to `sprBtnMenu` and import two images from the assets/UI folder—`btnMenu.png` and `btnMenu_over.png`.

Go back to the Sprite Editor and click on the Left Released event to edit it. Remove the existing code in the event and replace it with the following code:

```
/// @description Handling menu button click

room_goto(rmMenu);
```

When the user clicks and releases the button, we go to the main menu of the game. To view up to this point in the project, please open the file gms2_ch03_04.yyz

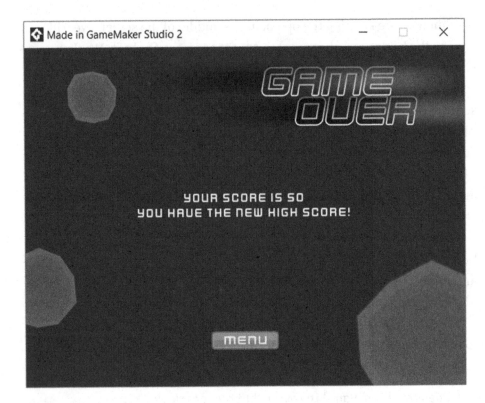

Figure 3-17. Game Over

Adding Music

Our game is well-rounded, but it lacks a bit of excitement. Let's fix that and add some music to make things interesting. Just like we added the sounds, start by creating a new Sound resource in the Resource Panel. Since this is a background score, we will rename it to bgmDistantStar.

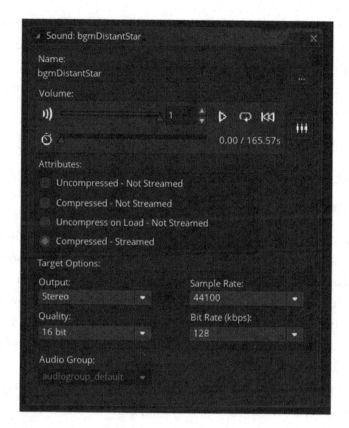

Figure 3-18. *Loading our background score*

Click the button next to the name of the resource to load our music file. Navigate to the assets/sound folder and import the mp3 file titled Distant_Star.mp3. Once the file is loaded, we will edit some attributes of the new sound resource we have just created. Right below where we edited the name of the resource, you will see a section for the sound's attributes. These decide how the sound resource should be treated when we export the game. We will set this to Compressed and Streamed, as our resource is going to be a large mp3 file, and we do not want to keep the file in memory, but rather decompress it and play it back in real time. Smaller resources like our explosion and laser firing sounds were kept as uncompressed, as they are smaller and do not take too much memory.

After creating the sound resource and loading the file, we will now play it back when the game starts. We already have a script that is executed in the Room Creation Code of the `rmInit` room; let's open it up and tell GMS to play our background score there. Open the `scrInitCreate` script from the Resources Panel and edit as given below.

```
global.highScore = 0;

audio_play_sound(bgmDistantStar, 100, true);

room_goto(rmMenu);
```

The only change here is the piece of code that tells GMS to play the audio. We use the `audio_play_sound()` function and pass it the sound resource that we want to play—in our case, the new sound resource we created with the mp3 file. The second parameter is the priority—we pass it to 100, telling GMS that this sound resource is off high priority. The third parameter tells GMS that this sound should be looped once it finishes playing, and that is it, we have finished our game!

Run the game to see it all in action. To view up to this point in the project, please open the file gms2_ch03_05.yyz.

Challenges

Now that we have created a small game, here are some challenges for that extends the game that we have built so far.

- Make the game juicier by adding sounds when you hover over buttons. In this challenge, you are required to bring our dull menus to life by adding sound effects to the button interactions.

- Add new enemy types that behave differently. In this challenge, you are required to add more enemy objects that behave differently from the enemy we currently have; the different enemies should have a different sprite as well as different behavior.

- Add other elements like meteorites that interfere with both player and enemies alike. In this challenge, you are required to add elements in the game with which you can interact, like meteorites and satellites; players as well as enemies will need to avoid them to stay alive.

CHAPTER 4

An Introduction to Node.js

In this chapter we focus on learning the basics of Node.js: what it is, what it can do for us, and how we can start to use it in game development. Node.js is a runtime environment that is used to execute JavaScript code, usually on the server side. It uses Chrome's V8 JavaScript engine internally, and hence it is well-maintained and extremely fast. Node.js uses an event-driven, non-blocking IO model that makes things fast as well as efficient. In simpler terms, node lets us execute JavaScript on servers, and it uses event-driven models very much like how events work on GameMaker Studio. Unlike other server-side software, node executes input and output operations parallel with one another and does not wait or block other operations while it performs I/O operations.

A simple Node.js server can act as an easy way to store information, do game logic, and much more. In our case, we will create a server that serves news to the players, stores high scores, and manages our multiplayer matches. Let's start by downloading and installing Node.js.

© Yadu Rajiv 2018
Y. Rajiv, *Developing Turn-Based Multiplayer Games*,
https://doi.org/10.1007/978-1-4842-3861-5_4

Installing Node.js

Installing Node.js is a very simple process. Open your browser and navigate to `https://nodejs.org`. Depending on your operating system, you will see a link to download both the *Long Time Support (LTS)* version as well as the *Current* stable version of Node.js. Click on the link to start your download of the LTS version, which is recommended for more stability. Once the download is complete, open the installer and follow the instructions to finish installing Node.js on your computer. Once node is installed, open your command prompt (or terminal) and type in the following to see the current version of Node.js installed:

```
# node -v
```

Your First Program

Node.js is essentially JavaScript without the browser and the Document Object Model (DOM) the browser offers. One of the simplest things one can do is to output data onto the console. You do that by using the global console object, which outputs to your standard output—in our case, the command line or terminal. The console object has many functions, one of which is the log function, which lets you log on to the terminal. Let us see it in action. Open your text editor and type in the code from Listing 4-1.

Listing 4-1. Code from hello.js

```
console.log("hello hello!");
```

Save the file as `hello.js`. Open your command prompt on Windows or the terminal on a Mac, navigate to where you saved the file, and execute the file using node.

```
# node hello.js
hello hello
```

Accessing the File System

One of the most common things to do with Node is to work with the file system. We will find ourselves constantly accessing files and folders, reading and writing to them as we go. Node.js makes it easy for us via the filesystem module. Let us explore two of the main functions that let you access and read data from a file and, in doing so, try to understand how Node.js fundamentally works asynchronously.

Synchronous functions are blocking, which means exactly that. They block the flow of execution of your code until the current blocking function is complete. In most cases, this is perfectly fine and expected, but what if you still can work and continue doing other functions while waiting for a particular action to finish? Most of the modern web today functions asynchronously; Node.js brings it to the server side.

What we try to do in Listing 4-2 is to access a file called news.txt, which contains three lines of text, read it, number them, and display it on the console. In the first example we will focus on loading files synchronously.

Listing 4-2. Code from newsSync.js

```
// load the file system module
var fs = require("fs");

// read the file synchronously
var data = fs.readFileSync("news.txt", "utf8");

// our file contains news, each news item split into multiple
lines
var news = data.split("\n");

// we print each news item to the console
for(var i=0; i<news.length; i++) {
        console.log(`${i+1}. ${news[i]}`);
}
```

In this example, we start off with creating a variable that loads the filesystem module (fs). We then use the readFileSync() function to read the file in a synchronous manner. What this means is that the program/server will wait until the file is completely loaded into memory before moving to the next line of execution. This means that everything that depends on the resolution of this action will have to wait until this file-read action is over. Depending on how big the file is, your wait times can vary. Most synchronous functions have a "Sync" attached to their function names.

In the readFileSync() function, the first parameter is the name of the file to be read, and the second parameter can be a string or an object, specifying the files' encoding—in this case, utf8—as we are reading a text file, as well as other flags. By default, the read flag 'r' is used. If no encoding is specified, the file is loaded into a Buffer object, which will then need to be read and converted manually.

Let us rewrite the same example so that it is asynchronous (see Listing 4-3). Instead of the readFileSync() function, we will use the readFile() function. The biggest difference is the addition of the third parameter in the function. The third parameter is a callback function, which gets called by Node.js as and when the file is read. The callback receives two parameters: an error object as well as the data that was read from the file. When we execute the code using node the contents of the files will be displayed as seen in Lising 4-4.

Listing 4-3. Code from news.js

```
// load the file system module
var fs = require("fs");

// read the data asynchronously
var data = fs.readFile("news.txt", "utf8",
fileFinishedReading);
```

```
// callback function to be called once the file is done loading
function fileFinishedReading(err, data) {

// in case of an error reading the file, throw the error and
stop the program
        if(err) throw err;

// our file contains news, each news item split into multiple lines
        var news = data.split("\n");

// we print each news item to the console
        let i=0;
        news.forEach((e) => {
                i += 1;
                console.log(`${i}. ${e}`);
});
}
```

Listing 4-4. Output from news.js

```
# node news.js
1. New characters and abilities will be available soon.
2. Interview with the developers are up now on the blog!
3. Share your SpaceLudo story with us!
```

The *news.txt* file needs to be in the same directory as the news.js file when you execute it via Node.js.

Both readFileSync() and readFile() work in a similar manner. In the synchronous example, the processing of the text and printing it onto the console starts only after the readFileSync() function finishes reading the file. In the second case, the execution continues in the next command. When the file has been read, the callback is executed. This type of callback and event-driven programming is the preferred way of working whenever possible as well as forms the fundamental building blocks of Node.js.

Extending Our News Loader Example

Let us extend our example from Listing 4-3 to load all text files in a given folder and print out the results. Similarly to our example in Listing 4-3, we will use asynchronous methods to read the folder, get a list of all the files, evaluate if it is a text file, and, if it is, load the contents into memory (see Listing 4-5).

Listing 4-5. Output from allnews.js

```
var fs = require("fs");
var path = require("path");

// our news folder
var newsFolder = __dirname + "/news/";

// an array to hold our text files
var newsFiles = [];

// read our news directory using readdir
fs.readdir(newsFolder, "utf8", (err, files) => {
        // section - 1 - getting the files
        // for each file in the folder, check if it is a text
        file and save it to our array
        files.filter((file) => {
                if(path.extname(file).toLowerCase() == ".txt")
{
                        newsFiles.push(file);
                }
        });

        // section - 2 - reading the files and displaying an
        output to the console
        // for each file in our array, read its contents and
        print each line to the console
```

```
newsFiles.forEach((file) => {
        fs.readFile(`${newsFolder}${file}`, "utf8",
        (err, data) => {
                data.split("\n").forEach((line) => {
                        console.log(line);
                });
        });
});
});
```

The first thing you will notice is that we are using an extra module called the path module. This module provides handy functions to extract data from file paths. We use it here to check if the file is a text file and has a .txt extension. The text files are placed inside a directory called news, which is in the same folder where the script resides.

The code can be primarily broken up into two sections. The first part of the script is where you will read the news directory using the fs.readdir() function. This function takes in a directory you want to read as the first parameter; the second parameter is an object that contains options usually an encoding for the data returned and a flag (read, write, etc.). The third parameter is the callback function that gets called when the files are read. In the example in Listing 4-5, the callback function takes an error parameter and a second variable for the list of files. The list of files is returned as an array of strings.

We use the path module and the extname() function to extract the extension from the filenames in the files list. We loop through the list of files and check if each file has a .txt extension. If it does, we will store the file name into an array for later use.

In the second part of this script, we loop through the list of files with a .txt extension and use the fs.readFile() function to read each of the files asynchronously like we have done before. As each file is read, we split the data returned into lines and print them onto the console.

Listing 4-6. Output from allnews.js

```
# node allnews.js
New characters and abilities will be available soon.
Share your SpaceLudo story with us!
SpaceLudo has new themes!
Interview with the developers are up now on the blog!
Balancing units, a deeper look.
```

Creating a Simple Server

Let us try creating something a bit more complex, like a server. A web server is usually a program that runs independently once it starts and interacts with clients that connect to it via a network. Servers in the context of games allow players to communicate with each other and play multiplayer games with each other by being the middle man helping in match-making as well as keeping all game session data in sync with all the players that are connected.

Let us jump right in by creating a simple server in Node.js. Being modular in nature, all of Node's core features are separated into modules that need to be added to each of your projects. So far, we have been using the file system (fs) module as well as the path module in our previous examples. External modules can be installed via the Node Package Manager (npm). In all our examples, we will use only the modules that come with Node.js and will not require you to install any new modules.

In this example, we will create a server that listens to a particular port on your computer for any new connections. When a connection is requested, we send out some data to whoever requested the connection. To make things easy, Node has a handy module that can handle Hypertext Transfer Protocol (HTTP) requests, called the http module. We will use the http module to create our server.

Listing 4-7. Code from http_example.js

```
// we import the http module
var http = require("http");

/*
// We create the server.
// The createServer function takes a function with two
parameters;
// a request and a response object.
*/
let server = http.createServer(function(req, res) {
res.writeHead(200, {'Content-Type':'text/plain'});
res.write("Hello Hello\n");

// end the response with an optional message
res.end("Bye bye");
});

// ask the server to listen to requests coming on port 8080
server.listen(8080);
```

We use the special function require() to load the http module
for us to use. We then use the http object to create a new server. The
createServer() function takes in a callback function that is executed
when a new connection request is made. This callback function will be
called with two parameters, one a request object and one a response
object. The request object contains information regarding the request itself
and also the person making the request. The response object is a stream to
which we write our data. Think of it like a file or data that we will send to
whoever made the request.

HTTP has set rules and structures that one needs to abide by when
working with it. The first part of all HTTP responses will have to be a
header, which tells the connected client what has happened and also

what kind of data is being sent. In our case, we use the writeHead()
function to send a response status code of 200, which tells the client that
the connection request has been accepted and everything is OK. We also
pass in an object that tells the client what type of content it should expect.
In our case, we have instructed the client to expect plain text data. After
writing (sending) the response header, we proceed to pass on a message
using the write() function. We conclude the response by calling the end()
function for the response stream object. We pass an optional message at
the end via the end() function as well. Once the server is created, we ask it
to listen for new connections on our computer on the specified port.

Save this file with a js extension—for example, save the file as
http_example.js. To run the newly created server, open a command
prompt or terminal. Type in node, followed by your file name, and hit
enter to start your server.

```
# node http_example.js
```

Once the server is started, open a new browser window and navigate to
either http://127.0.0.1:8080 or http://localhost:8080, both of which
should show you a response from our server.

Combining Our Server With File IO

Let us expand on our previous example by combining it with file reading
abilities. Instead of just passing data via HTTP, we will read our news files
from the folder and then pass the data to the client who requested
(see Listing 4-8).

Listing 4-8. Code from news_server.js

```
var fs = require("fs");
var path = require("path");
var http = require("http");
```

```
// our news folder
var newsFolder = __dirname + "/news/";

// an array to hold our text files
var newsFiles = [];

// all news data
var news = [];

// getting ready to read files
console.log("reading files...")

// read our news directory using readdir
fs.readdir(newsFolder, "utf8", (err, files) => {
// for each file in the folder, check if it is a text file and
save it to our array
        files.filter((file) => {
                if(path.extname(file).toLowerCase() == ".txt")
{
                        newsFiles.push(file);
                }
        });

// for each file in our array, read its contents and saves data
to our news variable
newsFiles.forEach((file) => {
fs.readFile(`${newsFolder}${file}`, "utf8", (err, data) => {
data.split("\n").forEach((item)=>{
news.push(item);
});
});
});
```

```
// done reading news, starting files
console.log("starting server...");

// once all news is loaded, we start our server.
startServer();
});

function startServer() {
let server = http.createServer(function(req, res) {
res.writeHead(200, {'Content-Type':'text/plain'});

news.forEach((item)=>{
res.write(`${item}\n`);
});

res.end();
});

// ask the server to listen to requests coming on port 8080
server.listen(8080);
console.log("server started at http://localhost:8080");
}
```

In this example, we combine the last two examples to create a server that serves all the news to a client who connects to the server. The script reads and loads the data and stores it into a news string. When a client requests a new connection, we pass the news back as a response, instead of our custom hello message. One major difference is that we have put the server creation code inside a function. We do so to activate the server only once the files have been successfully read and loaded into memory. Once the files are read, we call the startServer() function and the server is created, and we start to listen for incoming connections.

A Server With Multiple Paths

In the next example (see Listing 4-9), let us build upon our previous one but give the client the ability to navigate to different path. What this means is that when the player calls the root directory, the player is greeted with a message that tells them that they should look at the /news directory for more news. If any other path is requested, we fail and give the user a 404 status code, which means that we could not find the resource or URL the player was looking for.

Listing 4-9. Code from newspath_server.js

```
var fs = require("fs");
var path = require("path");
var http = require("http");
var parser = require("url");

// our news folder
var newsFolder = __dirname + "/news/";

// an array to hold our text files
var newsFiles = [];

// all news data
var news = [];

// getting ready to read files
console.log("reading files...")

// read our news directory using readdir
fs.readdir(newsFolder, "utf8", (err, files) => {

// for each file in the folder, check if it is a text file and
save it to our array
        files.filter((file) => {
```

```
            if(path.extname(file).toLowerCase() == ".txt") {
                newsFiles.push(file);
            }
    });

// for each file in our array, read its contents and saves data
to our news variable
    newsFiles.forEach((file) => {
            fs.readFile(`${newsFolder}${file}`, "utf8",
            (err, data) => {
                    data.split("\n").forEach((item)=>{
                        news.push(item);
                    });
            });
    });

// done reading news, starting files
    console.log("starting server...");

// once all news is loaded, we start our server.
    startServer();
});

function startServer() {
        let server = http.createServer(function(req, res) {
                // we parse the incoming request url
                var url = parser.parse(req.url, true);

// we check if the path name is something that we can use and
respond accordingly
                if(url.pathname == "/") {
                        res.writeHead(200, {'Content-
                        Type':'text/html'});
```

```
                        res.write('Welcome to the news
                        server<br />');
res.write('Go to <a href="/news">news</a> for more news.');
                } else if(url.pathname == "/news") {
                        res.writeHead(200, {'Content-
                        Type':'text/html'});
                        res.write("<ol>");
                        news.forEach((item)=>{
                                res.write(`<li>${item}</li>`);
                        });
                        res.write("</ol>");
                } else {
                        res.writeHead(404, {'Content-
                        Type':'text/html'});
                        res.write("Resource not found");
                }
                res.end();
        });
// ask the server to listen to requests coming on port 8080
        server.listen(8080);
        console.log("server started at http://localhost:8080");
}
```

The URL module helps us to parse the URL contained inside the initial request variable req, which is part of the callback in createServer(). The request object has a URL parameter, req.url, that contains the URL and its parts. The URL module breaks the URL and lets us access the component parts easily.

Once the initial URL is broken down, we can access the path using the pathname (url.pathname) property of the parsed URL object. Now that we know what path the user requested, we could respond appropriately. In the case of the root path "/" we respond with a welcome message as HTML text (Figure 4-1).

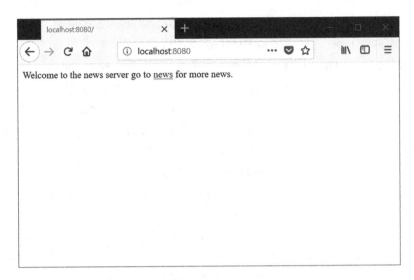

Figure 4-1. *Accessing our server from a browser. The server responds with a welcome message.*

If the user requested the "/news" path, we send them an ordered list of all the news we had loaded (Figure 4-2).

Figure 4-2. *A news request made, retrieves a list of news items from the server*

If the user requests anything other than the root or the news paths, we respond with a 404-status code and tell the user that the resource that they have requested cannot be accessed (Figure 4-3). You can add more resource path names using this method and create a custom HTTP API this way.

Figure 4-3. *If we try to access a path that we had not created in the server, we find our error message displayed*

Challenges

Now that we have learned how to read files, create a server, and communicate with clients in a meaningful way, here are some challenges for you to try.

- All the folders and files. In this challenge, you are required to read from all the files and subfolders in the news folder and display all available news. Your news folder can contain more folders and files inside them; your goal is to read from all the text files from within the news folder and all subfolders.

- All the paths. In this challenge, you are required to create multiple paths that sort and organize the results before returning it to the user.

CHAPTER 5

Talking to Your Server

In this chapter, we will focus on reading the news from our server using GameMaker Studio's network capabilities. Until now, we have been using a browser to get our information, but now, we will create a new project in GameMaker and try to read the news from inside our game.

Starting the Project

Start by creating a new project and a new object called objNewsReader. Once the news reader object is created, we will wait for 1 second before trying to connect to the server to read the news. We do so in order to let GameMaker start the game properly. Once you have created the object, add a create event and set an alarm to room_speed so that the alarm will be called in 1 second. Next, create a variable to hold the news text and temporarily set it to a string that gives the user a loading status message "loading news." (see Listing 5-1)

Listing 5-1. Create Event for objNewsReader

```
/// @description News reader and display object

// set the alarm to be called in 1 second
alarm[0] = room_speed;

// a default value for our news text display
displayText = "loading news...";
```

© Yadu Rajiv 2018
Y. Rajiv, *Developing Turn-Based Multiplayer Games*,
https://doi.org/10.1007/978-1-4842-3861-5_5

Let us add a Draw Event and display the text stored in the displayText variable (see Listing 5-2). We align the text horizontally and vertically to the center and middle, respectively, and draw the contents of the variable displayText at the x- and y-coordinates of the object.

Listing 5-2. Draw Event for objNewsReader

```
/// @description draw news text

// draws our news text
draw_set_halign(fa_center);
draw_set_valign(fa_middle);
draw_text(x, y, displayText);
```

For this to work, we need to drag and drop the object into the room. Let's keep it somewhere in the middle of the room toward the top. Next, we will retrieve the news from the server. Add an Alarm 0 event to objNewsReader and add the code from Listing 5-3 to it.

Listing 5-3. Alarm 0 Event for objNewsReader

```
/// @description load news from server

// send a request to our server
requestID = http_get("http://127.0.0.1:8080/news");
```

We use the http_get method to send an HTTP GET request from the URL we have specified the same way a browser would. Just like the browser as a client, our game client will receive the same kind of a response. The network events in GameMaker Studio are asynchronous just like NodeJS. Once we call the http_get method, we are required to wait for an asynchronous event, which is emitted when the response arrives.

Let's add an Asynchronous event for objNewsReader. From the list of available events under Asynchronous, select Async-HTTP. Within the event, add the code from Listing 5-4.

Listing 5-4. Async-HTTP Event for objNewsReader

```
/// @description Get our news

// is this the result for the request we made
if(ds_map_find_value(async_load, "id") == requestID) {
        if(ds_map_find_value(async_load, "status") == 0) {
                    displayText = ds_map_find_value(async_load,
                    "result");
        } else if(ds_map_find_value(async_load, "status") == 1) {
                displayText = "Downloading... please wait!";
        } else {
                displayText = "Sorry, unable to load news at
                this time.";
        }
}
```

When an Asynchronous event is emitted, any response or data that is loaded is saved onto a global ds_map called `async_load`. This variable is only available within the scope of asynchronous events and has a value of -1 at all other times. The `ds_map` is like an associative array, it stores data as a pair of keys and values. The easiest way to retrieve a value from a `ds_map` is to use the `ds_map_find_value` function.

When an HTTP event is triggered for an object, the `async_load` variable will contain a set of keys and values in the form of a `ds_map`. The request id that was returned during your http call is stored under key `id`, the state under the key `status` with a value less than 0 if there was an error, with a value of 1 if the operation is still in progress, or with a value of 0 if the operation has completed successfully. The response data from the server will be stored in the `result` key.

In our event above, we first check if the requestID is the same as the `id` in the value returned (we check this since this event is triggered for multiple HTTP events). Then we check if the `status` is 0 and hence successful, and finally, we take the response contained in the result and save it into the displayText variable. If, for some reason, the operation wasn't successful, display a different message to the player. In case the data from the server is large and it takes time downloading it, the status will be of the value 1.

Apart from these values we have used, the ds_map also contains a url, which is the complete URL we have requested as well as a raw HTTP status code in http_status (if available).

Let us see this in action. Be sure to run our last created example file as shown in Listing 5-5. Once the server is up and running, run the GameMaker Studio project.

Listing 5-5. Execute Our Server

```
# node newspath_server.js
```

Once the program loads, you may notice that the news doesn't appear as we might have expected. Currently our server returns data that contains HTML that do not need and cannot parse. Let us go back and edit our server so that we can get our news in plain text and with line breaks instead of HTML tags. Open newspath_server.js and scroll down to the startServer function; add an if condition so that you can handle a new path (see Listing 5-6).

Listing 5-6. Partial Code from newspath_server2.js

```
...

function startServer() {

  let server = http.createServer(function(req, res) {

    // we parse the incoming request url
    var url = parser.parse(req.url, true);
```

```
// we check if the path name is something that we can use
and respond accordingly
if(url.pathname == "/") {
  res.writeHead(200, {'Content-Type':'text/html'});
  res.write('Welcome to the news server go to
  <a href="/news">news</a> for more news.');
} else if(url.pathname == "/news") {
  res.writeHead(200, {'Content-Type':'text/html'});
  res.write("<ol>");
  news.forEach((item)=>{
    res.write(`<li>${item}</li>`);
  });
  res.write("</ol>");
} else if(url.pathname == "/plain") {
  res.writeHead(200, {'Content-Type':'text/plain'});
  news.forEach((item)=>{
    res.write(`${item}\n`);
  });
} else {
  res.writeHead(404, {'Content-Type':'text/html'});
  res.write("Resource not found");
}

  res.end();

});

// ask the server to listen to requests coming on port 8080
server.listen(8080);
console.log("server started at http://localhost:8080");

}
```

In the startServer function, we check if the url.pathname is "/plain", and if it is, we return a status of 200 (for success) and set the content type as text/plain. In the next line we loop through each item in the news array and write it onto our response object along with a line break.

In our GameMaker Studio project, let us open up our objNewsReader object and navigate to the Alarm 0 event where we call our server. We change our request path to our new path to retrieve the news as plain text (see Listing 5-7).

Listing 5-7. Alarm 0 Event for objNewsReader

```
/// @description load news from server

// send a request to our server
requestID = http_get("http://127.0.0.1:8080/plain");
```

Explore the code in the file - gms2_ch05_01.yyz.

Going Beyond Web APIs

In the previous example, we looked at the HTTP module and how to use it to create to a web server and a web-based API to retrieve news. Now, with the help of the net module, we will explore how to open a constant communication channel. The net module provides an asynchronous network API for creating stream-based TCP servers and clients. The game that we will be creating will make use of GameMaker Studio's built in networking functions to create a constant connection with our server.

We will create a framework that will allow us to quickly send messages back and forth between the server and our game client. Let us start by creating a small die rolling application; when the server gets a request form the client to roll a die, the server will roll a die and send the result back to the client. The major difference between our web API and the new model is that we will connect with the server at the start of the game and keep that connection open until we quit the game. Let us start again with a smaller chunk of the program before we create our framework.

We will first create a small server using NodeJS that will connect to any incoming connection using the net module, and we will send an array of text to any client who connects. We will first test it using a telnet client and then recreate the same using GameMaker Studio. Let us jump headfirst into the code for our server (see Listing 5-8).

Listing 5-8. Code from netServer_simple_start.js

```
// import the net module
const net = require("net");

// the port and address that our server will be on
const PORT = 5836;
const ADDRESS = "";

// create our server and pass the callback to be called when a
client connects
let server = net.createServer(onClientConnected);
// start listening for requests on our port and address
server.listen(PORT, ADDRESS);

// callback function for handling connections
function onClientConnected(socket) {

        // set the encoding for data on this socket to text
        socket.setEncoding('utf8');

        // log a message when a new client connects
        var clientName = `${socket.remoteAddress}:${socket.
        remotePort}`
        console.log(`New client connected: ${clientName}`);
```

```
    // set a callback to handle data form clients
    socket.on('data', onClientData);

        // set a callback to handle client disconnection
        socket.on('end', onClientDisconnected);

}

// callback for when a client sends us some data
function onClientData(message) {
        console.log(`Client says: ${message}`);
        this.write("hello friend.");
}

// callback for when a client disconnects
function onClientDisconnected() {
        var clientName = `${this.remoteAddress}:${this.
        remotePort}`
        console.log(`${clientName} disconnected.`);
}

// log our server details when the server starts
console.log(`Server started at ${ADDRESS}:${PORT}`);
```

This server is very similar to our previous HTTP server and how it is constructed. We import the net module and use the createServer function to create our server. Once our server is created just like our old HTTP server, we listen in for any requests via an address and a port. The createServer functions take in some options and, more importantly, a function that will be called when a new connection is established. In our example above in Listing 5-8, we pass onClientConnected via the createServer method, and this is called when anyone tries to connect to the server.

Let us run this server and try to connect to it via telnet. Open up the command prompt (or terminal) and type in the following to start the server:

```
# node netServer_simple_start.js
```

Once you start the server, you should see a message similar to what is given below.

```
Server started at 127.0.0.1:5836
```

Open up a new command prompt and type in the following and hit enter. We will try to use telnet to connect to our server.

```
# telnet 127.0.0.1 5836
```

Once the connection is established you should see a positive response, as shown here, in the telent application.

```
Trying 127.0.0.1...
Connected to localhost.
Escape character is '^]'.
```

At the same time, in the previous terminal window, you will notice that a new connection has been established in the server.

```
New client connected: 127.0.0.1:61987
```

When a new client connects to our server, the onClientConnected function is called, and a net.Socket object for the incoming connection is passed to it. Each new client connected will have a distinct socket, and we will be using this socket to communicate back with the clients. In our onClientConnected function, we first set the socket's encoding to text, instructing it that all data coming in will be strings. The details of our client's ip address as well as the port through which they are connecting are then printed on to the console, as we saw earlier. We then go on to add two event handlers, onClientData and onClientDisconnected, on the newly connected socket. The onClientData function will handle any data that will be sent to the server, and the onClientDisconnected function will be called when a client disconnects from the server. Let us go back to our telnet client and send a message to our server and see what happens. Go back to the terminal window where you opened telnet before; if it is still running, type in any text and hit enter.

```
Trying 127.0.0.1...
Connected to localhost.
Escape character is '^]'.
hello
hello friend.
```

When I typed in hello and pressed enter, the server responded with a message, "hello friend." let us check our server.

```
New client connected: 127.0.0.1:61987
Client says: hello
```

Our server has received the message we have sent, and it displays it on the terminal window. When a client sends in any data, the data event for the socket is emitted and the onClientData function is called. The data passed into the function will be a buffer or a string—in our case, a string. We print out the message that the server receives, like we see above.

Let us disconnect our telnet client from our server and see what happens. Close the terminal in which the telnet client is running or exit out to the telnet menu using the escape character, if any. In our case, we have to press the control key and then the closing square bracket keys (Ctrl+]) to exit to the telnet menu prompt. In the telnet menu, type in "quit" to close the connection.

```
127.0.0.1:61987 disconnected.
```

If we go back to our server, which is still running, you can see that it displays that our telnet client was disconnected.

124

The Die Roller Server

Before we move on, let us modify our new server so that it can take in some commands from clients. Let us modify the server so that every time we ask the server to "roll" it will roll a die and give us the result. Everything about this new server is the same as the previous one, except that we will now check, evaluate, and respond to each message that comes in to the server. Listing 5-9 shows how we will modify the data event so as to respond to client messages.

Listing 5-9. Partial Code from netServer_simple_dice.js

```
// callback for when a client sends us some data
function onClientData(message) {

        // trim the data so that there are no empty spaces or
        line breaks etc
        var data = message.trim();

        console.log(`Client says: ${data}`);

        // roll a 1d6
        if(data == "roll") {
                var r = Math.floor((Math.random()*6)+1).toString();
                 this.write(`${r}\n`);
        } else {
                this.write(`you said "${data}"\n`);
        }

}
```

In the onClientData function, we check if the data we received via the argument was "roll", and if it was, we use the Math.random function to generate a random. The number will then be written back using the write method, which is part of the socket. Run this server and connect to it via telnet as we did earlier. We trim the data just in case it has extra spaces or hidden characters, such as line breaks, etc. When we are writing back in this example, it is good to note that we are ending our strings with a new line character that will be parsed by telnet when displaying the data.

```
# node netServer_simple_dice.js
Server started at 127.0.0.1:5836
```

And once it starts, connect to the server via telnet.

```
# telnet 127.0.0.1 5836
Trying 127.0.0.1...
Connected to localhost.
Escape character is '^]'.
```

Like before we will be able to see that a new client was connected to the server.

```
New client connected: 127.0.0.1:50821
```

Go back to the telnet client and type in roll to see our code in action.

```
# telnet 127.0.0.1 5836
Trying 127.0.0.1...
Connected to localhost.
Escape character is '^]'.
roll
2
roll
3
roll
6
hello
you said "hello"
roll
3
```

Our server would reflect the same actions just like before.

```
# node netServer_simple_dice.js
Server started at 127.0.0.1:5836
New client connected: 127.0.0.1:50943
Client says: roll
Client says: roll
Client says: roll
Client says: hello
Client says: roll
```

Talking to Our Die Roller Server via GameMaker Studio

Now that we have made a server and see it in action via our telnet client, let us see how we can do the same via GameMaker Studio. Our approach will be similar to that of our previous method, when we used http functions, but the major difference is that will use the other networking functions rather than the previously used http functions.

Our GameMaker application will be very close to what the telnet client did. We will first connect to the server; once that connection is established, we will ask it to roll the die. Once we get a value from the server, we will display it to the player.

Create a new GameMaker Studio project. We are going to have two objects in our room:

- A network manager object that will do all the communicating

- A die object with a dice sprite attached to it

The network manager object that we will create will initialize the connection as well as help communicate with the server. Once the communication is established, whenever we click on the die, we send a request to the server and the server communicates the die value back. Depending on the value, we change the dice object.

Let us start by importing the die sprite; create a new sprite from images and import the red die images in the assets folder for the chapter. Once all the images are inside one sprite, make sure the origin is in set to Middle Center (by default this may be set to Top Left) from the options available for the sprite. Change the animation speed to 12. Once this is done, create an object for the die and call it objDie. Attach the die sprite we created earlier. Drag and drop a copy of the object into the middle of our room. On the objDie object, add a create event, as shown in Listing 5-10.

Listing 5-10. Create Event for objDie

```
/// @description Init dice

// center the die in the middle of the room
x = room_width/2;
y = room_height/2;

// stop animations
image_speed = 0;

// set the value of the die
global.dieValue = 1;

// set the current index of the sprite sub image
image_index = global.dieValue - 1;
```

We set the x- and y-position of the die to the center of the room, and we stop all animations. We then create a new global variable called global.dieValue, which will hold the value of the current die. At the moment we set it to 1. We reduce one from the value of the die and set it to the image_index property of the sprite attached to the object. As we have already seen, the image_index is the index of the subimage inside the sprite, and the index values start from 0.

Create a Mouse - Left Released event for objDie and add the code in Listing 5-11 to it. We will modify this later when we have our network manager object up and running. For the moment, if objDie is not animating, when the user clicks on it, we start the animation. Explore the code in the file gms2_ch05_02_01.yyz.

Listing 5-11. Mouse - Left Released Event

```
/// @description Click event handler

if(image_speed == 0) {
        image_speed = 1;
}
```

Creating the network manager object is our next step, and since we don't need any sprites for it, let us start by creating a new object. Once you create the objNetworkManager object, add two variables to it—one for the port that we will connect to (set to 5836) and the other, the address we will connect to. We will set the address to 127.0.0.1 and change its type to a String. Next, add a Create event to the objNetworkManager object and add the code from Listing 5-12 to it.

Listing 5-12. Create Event for objNetworkManager

```
/// @description Setup our network manager

global.nmSocket = -1;

// tell gamemaker to timeout this connection if there is no
response in 4000ms (4 seconds)
network_set_config(network_config_connect_timeout, 4000);
```

```
// tell gamemaker to use a non-blocking socket connection
network_set_config(network_config_use_non_blocking_socket, true);

// create a socket connection
global.nmSocket = network_create_socket(network_socket_tcp);

// connect to the remote socket
network_connect_raw(global.nmSocket, address, port);
```

There is a lot happening here; let us go through it line by line. At the onset, we declare a global variable to store the socket we will be creating. Think of the socket as a connection between our game and the server. In the future, we will be using this socket to communicate with the server. But first, we need to configure our network settings.

The network_set_config function takes in two variables: the first is a constant we use to designate what value we want to set, and the second is the new value we want. We use it to set two settings; in the first case, we set the network_config_connect_timeout setting to 4000. What this does is tell GameMaker that if we don't get a response from the server in 4 seconds, then we should not wait for it and tell the user that the allotted time is over.

The second is the network_config_use_non_blocking_socket setting that we set to true. This tells GameMaker studio to not wait for the network connection to be complete and continue processing other information (like drawing the screen or objects, etc).

Our next step is to create the socket that we will use to communicate with the server. We use the network_create_socket function to create a new socket. A new socket id is returned, and we will save it away in the global we have created for later use. We tell GameMaker that we want to create a TCP socket by passing in the constant network_socket_tcp. Once the socket is created, we will use it to connect to our server.

The networking functions, aside from the http functions, are primarily meant to be used between applications created with GameMaker Studio. What I mean by that is the most common approach to create a server–client system would be to create both the game server and the game client using GameMaker Studio. But since we are using NodeJS to create our server, we will not be using the common networking functions.

We will be using the network_connect_raw function to connect, via the socket we have just created, to the IP address and port that we specified as variables. Similarly to the http functions from our previous examples, these networking functions are also asynchronous in nature and will have to wait for GameMaker to trigger the asynchronous events for our objNetworkManager object. Under the Asynchronous events for objNetworkManager, add an Async-Networking event. This event will be the core of all our network communications, as all messages from the server will be passed to this event. This means when a connection with the server is established through the network_connect_raw function we had called earlier, we will get a response here. Let us first write the code to handle the events and then delve into explanations (see Listing 5-13).

Listing 5-13. Async-Networking Event for objNetworkManager

```
/// @description Handle network messages

// get the type of network event that has happened
type = async_load[? "type"];

switch(type)
{
        // we have connected to the server
        case network_type_non_blocking_connect:

                // check if we actually succeeded in connecting
                to the server
                if(async_load[? "succeeded"]) {
                        global.nmStatus = "connection successful";
                        objDie.visible = true;
```

```
        } else {
                global.nmStatus = "connection failed!";
        }

        show_debug_message(global.nmStatus);

        break;

    // unhandled or unknown events.
    default:

        show_debug_message("uncaught network event!");

        break;

}
```

The Async-Networking event of objNetworkManager is where all
the action happens. As soon as we connect to the server, the Async-
Networking event is triggered. As this event is triggered for multiple types
of server events, we are first required to check what specific type of event
was triggered. We do so by checking in a globally accessible ds_map
variable called async_load. The async_load ds_map is a global variable,
but it will only be filled with data during an Async-Networking event. To
quickly understand what the async_load variable contains, let us use the
json_encode function to convert the ds_map into a JSON string. When we
connect to the server and the Async-Networking event is triggered, the data
returned via the async_load variable looks like what you see in Listing 5-14.

Listing 5-14. The Contents of the async_load During the Connection

```
{ "succeeded": 1.000000, "ip": "127.0.0.1", "port": 5836.000000,
"socket": 0.000000, "type": 4.000000, "id": 0.000000 }
```

The first variable that we are interested in is the type. The type determines the type of network event that has occurred. It can be one of four constants: network_type_connect (with a value 1); network_type_disconnect (with a value 2); network_type_data (with a value 3); and network_type_non_blocking_connect (with a value 4). Since we have configured GameMaker Studio to be non-blocking when connecting to a server, the type of event triggered here will the fourth one, the network_type_non_blocking_connect.

We use a switch statement to check if the current event type is network_type_non_blocking_connect and proceed to check if the map value for the variable succeeded was set to 1. If the connection was successful, the value of succeeded will be 1; if it was a failure, the value will be 0. If our connection was successful, then we set the visible property of the objDie instance to true. Open the objDie object in the object editor and change the visible property to false (uncheck the option), so that when the application loads and connects to the server successfully, the die is shown. Explore the code in the file gms2_ch05_02_02.yyz.

In our next step, we will try to receive data from the server.

Modifying Our Server for Sending Data to GMS2

Let us go back to our server and modify the on data event handler so that we can send more meaningful information to our GameMaker client. Let us rewrite the onClientData event handler so that it sends an array of information, which includes the initial request message from the client; this will help us differentiate the different kinds of messages we send to our server (see Listing 5-15).

Listing 5-15. Partial Code from netServer_simple_dice_gm.js

```
// callback for when a client sends us some data
function onClientData(message) {

        // trim the data so that there are no empty spaces or
        line breaks etc
        var data = message.trim();

        console.log(`Client says: ${data}`);

        // roll a 1d6
        if(data == "roll") {
                var r = Math.floor((Math.random()*6)+1).
                toString();
                this.write(JSON.stringify([data, r]));
                console.log(`Server rolls: ${r}`);
        } else {
                this.write(JSON.stringify([data, data]));
        }

}
```

The only change here is how and what data we write back to the client. The JavaScript Object Notation (JSON) object has methods that help us in parsing JSON as well as in converting to JSON. We use it to convert our array of information into a JSON string, which we can decode inside GameMaker. The first item in our array is always the message we received from the client, followed by our results. In the case of our roll message, the first item in the array returned will be "roll," and the second item will be the actual value from the die rolled. Save the file after you make your changes, and start the server.

Rolling the Die

Let us go back to GameMaker and our die roller application and try to send the roll command to the server when the user clicks on the objDie instance. Open the Left-Released event for the objDie object and make the changes shown in Listing 5-16.

Listing 5-16. Left-Released Event for objDie

```
/// @description Click event handler

if(image_speed == 0) {
        image_speed = 1;

        // create the buffer
        var _msg = "roll";
        var _buff = buffer_create(string_length(_msg), buffer_
        grow, 1);
        buffer_write(_buff, buffer_text, _msg);

        // send the message
        with(objNetworkManager) {
                network_send_raw(global.nmSocket, _buff,
                buffer_tell(_buff))
        }

        // cleanup
        buffer_delete(_buff);

}
```

There are three major sections of code here; let us examine them individually. In the first section once you click the objDie object, we go about preparing a special type of variable called the buffer. The buffer is a region in physical memory that is primarily used to hold data temporarily or when modifying it. In our case, we create a buffer variable to hold the message we are sending to the server. We will hold it in the buffer until we send it and delete it afterward.

To create and manipulate buffers, there are a number of functions prefixed with "buffer_". We will be using the buffer_create function to create a buffer of a specified size. The buffer_create function takes in three parameters: the size of a buffer, the type of the buffer, and a byte alignment. We will use the length of the text as the size of the buffer we are making, and for the second parameter, we will set it to the constant buffer_grow, which tells GameMaker Studio to resize the buffer as needed. The last property, which is byte alignment, varies depending on the type of data we are storing; for Strings, it should always be 1.

After we create a buffer, in the second section we go ahead and write our message on the buffer using the buffer_write function. Since there are many kinds of buffers, we need to explicitly state that we are writing a *string* type on the buffer by using the buffer_text constant as the second parameter. The third and last parameter in the buffer_write function is the actual data itself. Once the data is in the buffer, we can send it to our server.

In the third section, we will change our scope to the objNetworkManager instance using the with construction, since we want all network events to be captured by the Async-Networking event handler we created earlier. From inside the with construction we use the network_send_raw function to send the message to the server. The network_send_raw function takes three parameters: the socket through which we have connected to the server, the buffer with the data, and the size of the buffer. The easiest way to find the size of the buffer is to use the buffer_get_size function.

Now that we can send data, let's see if our server receives it. Make sure the server is running, and run the game. Once the game is loaded and our connection established, click on the now visible die to send the message. At the moment, the die will animate endlessly, but if we check our server, we can see that the data was received.

```
# node netServer_simple_dice_gm.js
Server started at 127.0.0.1:5836
New client connected: 127.0.0.1:51308
Client says: roll
Server rolls: 4
```

If we check our Output window in GameMaker Studio we can see this in action.

```
{ "succeeded": 1.000000, "ip": "127.0.0.1", "port": 5836.000000,
"socket": 0.000000, "type": 4.000000, "id": 0.000000 }
connection successful
{ "ip": "127.0.0.1", "port": 5836.000000, "buffer": 0.000000,
"size": 12.000000, "type": 3.000000, "id": 0.000000 }
```

Our Async-Networking event prints out the contents of the async_load during the data event, which lets us see that the first event was that of our client connecting to the server, and the second event has type variable with the value of 3, which makes it a network_type_data event. So we now know that we are sending a message to the server and getting some data back. In the next section, let us find out how we can read and interpret this data that is being sent back by the server. Explore the code so far in the file gms2_ch05_02_03.yyz.

Getting the Data

Now that we know that the data is being sent back to our game, we need to collect it and then set the die to the value we got from the server. To get the data, we need to change our Async-Networking event and edit our switch statement so that a network_type_data event can be handled (see Listing 5-17).

Listing 5-17. Async-Networking Event for objNetworkManager

```
/// @description Handle network messages

// get the type of network event that has happened
type = async_load[? "type"];

show_debug_message(json_encode(async_load));

switch(type)
{
        // we have connected to the server
        case network_type_non_blocking_connect:
                // check if we actually succeeded in connecting
                to the server
                if(async_load[? "succeeded"]) {
                        global.nmStatus = "connection successful";
                        objDie.visible = true;

                } else {
                        global.nmStatus = "connection failed!";
                }

                show_debug_message(global.nmStatus);

        break;

        case network_type_data:
                // getting the data from the buffer
                var data = "";
                var pos = buffer_tell(async_load[? "buffer"]);
                while(pos < async_load[? "size"]) {
                        data += buffer_read(async_load[?
                        "buffer"], buffer_text);
```

```
        pos = buffer_tell(async_load[? "buffer"]);
    }

    // decoding the data
    var resultMap = json_decode(data);
    var list = resultMap[? "default"];

    // reading the values
    if(ds_list_find_value(list, 0) == "roll") {
        global.dieValue = ds_list_find_
        value(list, 1);
        with(objDie) {
            image_speed = 0;
            image_index = floor(real(global.
            dieValue)) - 1;
        }
    }

    // cleanup
    ds_map_destroy(resultMap);

    break;

// unhandled or unknown events.
default:

    show_debug_message("uncaught network event!");

    break;

}
```

The biggest change is the addition of the case that handles the network_type_data type of event. This section can be broken into four parts. In the first part, we collate the data that has been sent to us; in the second, we parse the data; in the third, we read and set the value of the die; and in the fourth, we free up our memory and clean up. Let us go through each part one by one.

{ "ip": "127.0.0.1", "port": 5836.000000, "buffer": 0.000000, "size": 12.000000, "type": 3.000000, "id": 0.000000 }

First, let us examine the data we had collected in our Output window earlier, through which we determined that we were indeed being sent data. If we examine the data that was sent in the async_load variable during the data event, we see that there is a new element called buffer. This buffer holds the data that was sent by the server. Along with the buffer, we can see the size variable, which tells us exactly how big this buffer is. Armed with these two pieces of information, we loop through the buffer and collect all the data.

```
...
// getting the data from the buffer
var data = "";
var pos = buffer_tell(async_load[? "buffer"]);
while(pos < async_load[? "size"]) {
        data += buffer_read(async_load[? "buffer"], buffer_text);
        pos = buffer_tell(async_load[? "buffer"]);
}
```

The data variable will hold the complete data we receive from the server. The pos variable stores the current read position of the buffer (the current position from which data is being read). The buffer_tell function is used to retrieve the current read position of the buffer—at this moment, the beginning of the buffer. We loop until our buffer read position reaches the end, here designated by the size of the buffer. We use the buffer_read function to read the data from the buffer. The buffer_read function takes in a buffer as well as a type for the data that is being read. Each time we loop, we append the data that was read to the data variable. Each time we read data using the buffer_read function, the read position moves ahead. To find out how far ahead we have come, we use the buffer_tell function again. Once the data is read, we need to parse it.

```
// decoding the data
var resultMap = json_decode(data);
var list = resultMap[? "default"];
```

Since we know that the data coming in is a JSON string, we can use the json_decode function to parse that string and convert it into a ds_map. The json_decode function constructs ds_maps and ds_lists depending on how the data is structured. In our case, since we are receiving an array of information, the json_decode function constructs a ds_map with a single element inside, called default, with the values of the array as a ds_list. A ds_list can technically be used like an array.

```
// reading the values
if(string(ds_list_find_value(list, 0)) == "roll") {
        global.dieValue = floor(real(ds_list_find_value(list, 1)));
        with(objDie) {
                image_speed = 0;
                image_index = global.dieValue - 1;
        }
}
```

Once we have our list, we check if the first value (at index 0) is roll. If yes, then we extract the second value from the list, which is the actual value of the die roll. We convert the die roll value from a string to a number. In the next section, we use a with construction to change our scope to the objDie object and then change its image_speed to 0, stopping its animation and changing its image_index to our global.dieValue–1(since image_index is 0 indexed). Explore the code in the file gms2_ch05_02_04.yyz.

Challenges

Now that both GMS2 and Node.js can talk to each other and exchange information, try to extend the dieRoller server and the GameMaker Studio client as a challenge!

- Try to extend the server so that it can work for multiple dice. Currently we are rolling a 1d6, which means we are rolling one six-sided die. Could you extend it in such a way that you can roll a 2d6 (two six-sided die) or 1d20 (one twenty-sided die).

- Can you also find a way to delay the animation for at least 1 second before showing the result?

CHAPTER 6

Building the Multiplayer Game

This chapter will focus on creating a simple turn-based multiplayer game building on all the knowledge that we have gained through the exercises in the previous chapters. We will start by writing a simple flow chart to map out all the possible logical states and scenes for our game and then continue to work on building a simple server in NodeJS and a client using GameMaker Studio's network capabilities.

Since our last exercise focused on creating a die rolling application, we will build on top of it to create a simple die-based jeopardy game, much like Pig. The objective of the game is to be the first to reach a score of 100 or more. In each turn, players roll the die multiple times. Each time they roll during their turn, the die value is added to the turn total as long as the die rolled is not 1. After rolling, the player can decide to hold the current turn total, effectively adding it to their score and ending the turn, or roll yet another time. At any point during their turn, if the player rolls a 1, their turn total becomes 0, and their turn ends. The game ends when all players have finished their turns. Instead of following the pig as a symbol of greed, we will name our game The Jackal's Dice.

Since our goal is to explain clearly how both the server and client work, we will keep the game as simple as possible. This will also give you an opportunity to build upon the game and create more interesting features on top of it. We will break down all the details of both the client and the

© Yadu Rajiv 2018
Y. Rajiv, *Developing Turn-Based Multiplayer Games*,
https://doi.org/10.1007/978-1-4842-3861-5_6

server as bullet points so that we have a clear picture in our minds before starting our work.

The Client

1. Start Room: Connects to server

2. Visual

3. Image: Title of the game

4. Label: Connection status

5. Player Action

6. None

7. Logic

8. Game auto-connects to the server and waits for unique id for the player

9. Once a valid response is received, game continues to the main screen.

10. Main Room: Screen

11. Visual

12. Image: Title of the game

13. Button: Start a game with a player

14. Button: Exit Game

15. Player action

16. Start a new game by clicking on the Start Game button.

17. Quit game by clicking the Quit Game button.

18. Logic

19. None

20. Lobby Room: Waiting room

21. Visual

22. Label: Looking for players

23. Button: Return to Menu

24. Player action

25. Return to Menu and stop looking for other players

26. Logic

27. The game will wait until the server finds an opponent, starts a new match, and sends the match details.

28. Once the opponent and match details arrive, the player is taken to the game screen.

29. Game room

30. Visual

31. Button: Roll dice

32. Button: Hold

33. Label: Status message—current dice roll value, your score, current turn total, opponent's score

34. Player action

35. Players wait for their turn.

36. On their turn, players can roll the dice and wait for the result; depending on which, they can roll again, hold, or end their turn.

37. The hold button holds the current value and adds to the player's score and ends the player's turn.

38. Logic

39. If it is the player's turn, update the status message.

40. Disable and enable buttons depending on whose turn it is.

41. Game end

42. Label: Display last game's status

The Server

1. Waits for clients to connect

2. When a client connects, give them a unique id and store information about them in a clients list.

3. When a client disconnects, remove them from the clients list.

4. When a client requests for a match, find an opponent, create a match, change the client status, and send back the match details to both clients.

5. If the server can't find a match, wait for more opponents to join the system.

6. In game, listen to clients and processes messages from the client.

7. Roll dice.

8. Hold.

9. Score update: Updates players' scores and closes game when one player wins

Building the Server

We will start by creating our server. Our new server will be similar to the one we created in the previous chapter, but we will better organize it for reusability. We will start by refactoring the server code from the previous chapter. In our previous example where we created a dice roller application, we used a single JavaScript that acted as the server and handled all our messages to and from the client. This time around, we will separate out the logic so that we can better manage the application.

Our starting point will be a simple app.js file that will primarily contain the port and IP address used by our server as well as a code that will start our game server as seen in Listing 6-1.

Listing 6-1. Code from app.js

```
const GameServer = require("./GameServer.js");

// the port and address that our server will be on
const PORT = 5836;
const ADDRESS = "127.0.0.1";

// create our game server
let game = new GameServer(PORT, ADDRESS);

// log our server details when the server starts
console.log(`Server started at ${ADDRESS}:${PORT}`);
```

The actual game server code will be separated from this and will be written in GameServer.js as a separate node module. In app.js we will require it like we add modules, with a difference that we are loading the module from the same folder. We then create a new GameServer object by passing in the port and address that our server will use. Let us now take a deeper look at how our GameServer class works (see Listing 6-2).

Listing 6-2. Code from GameServer.js

```javascript
// import the net module
const net = require("net");
const crypto = require("crypto");
const Client = require("./Client.js");

module.exports = class GameServer {

  constructor(port, address) {
    this.port = port;
    this.address = address;

    // all our clients
    this.clients = [];

    // create our server and pass the callback to be called
    when a client connects
    this.server = net.createServer((socket) => this.
    onClientConnected(socket));

    // start listening for requests on our port and address
    this.server.listen(this.port, this.address);

  }

  // callback function for handling connections
  onClientConnected(socket) {

    // set the encoding for data on this socket to text
    socket.setEncoding('utf8');

    // generate a client id
    var clientID = getRandomID();

    // create a new client
    var client = new Client(clientID, socket);
```

```
  // log to console
  console.log(`New client connected: ${client.clientName}`);

  // welcome message with client id
  socket.write(JSON.stringify(["hello", client.id]));

  // add client to our clients list
  this.clients.push(client);

  console.log(`client count: ${this.clients.length}`);

  // clean up for the server when the client disconnects
  client.on('end', (client) => this.
  onClientDisconnected(client));

}

onClientDisconnected(client) {
  console.log(`${client.clientName} has disconnected!`);

  // remove the client from our clients list once it has been
  disconnected!
  var c = this.getIndexWithID(this.clients, client.id);
  if(c != -1) {
    this.clients.splice(c, 1);
  }

  console.log(`client count: ${this.clients.length}`);
}

// return the index of an item from an array if the item has
the given id
getIndexWithID(a, id) {
  return a.findIndex((c) => { return c["id"] === id});
}
```

```
// Returns a random unique ID to use for new players and games
getRandomID() {
  return crypto.randomBytes(16).toString('hex');
}

}
```

The GameServer class has three major functions: the constructor for the class, the onClientConnected, and onClientDisconnected functions. The constructor for the class is called when a new server object is created in the app.js file. The constructor takes two arguments: the port and address for the server. In the first lines of the constructor function, we store the port and address values onto the GameServer object itself through the this keyword (the this keyword in the current context refers to the GameServer object). We then initialize an empty array called "clients" that would eventually hold all new connections that our server makes.

```
// create our server and pass the callback to be called
when a client connects
this.server = net.createServer((socket) => this.
onClientConnected(socket));
```

We then create the server using the net module and use the new arrow function to redirect the callback to our class's onClientConnected() function. The arrow function is a new addition to JavaScript that helps us to quickly create an anonymous function and helps us access the GameServer class's onClientConnected() function through the this keyword. We then ask the server to listen for new connections on the port and IP address provided.

From the last example in the previous chapter, you will remember that the callback function receives a net.Socket object for the incoming connection. When a new connection is established, our server's onClientConnected() function is called. Before we explore this function in detail, we need to understand our Client class. Our Client class is essentially an extension of the EventEmitter class. The EventEmitter class will help us to easily emit events as well as make it easy for our GameServer class to listen to these events. Let us take a look at the Client.js file as seen in Listing 6-3 below and explore it quickly before returning to our GameServer.

Listing 6-3. Code from Client.js

```javascript
const EventEmitter = require('events');

class Client extends EventEmitter {
  constructor(id, socket) {
    super();

    this.id = id;
    this.room = "lobby";
    this.socket = socket;
    this.remoteAddress = socket.remoteAddress;
    this.remotePort = socket.remotePort;
    this.clientName = `${this.id}:${this.remoteAddress}:${this.
    remotePort}`;
    this.currentGameID = "";

    // set a callback to handle data form clients
    this.socket.on('data', (data) => this.onClientData(data));

    // set a callback to handle client disconnection
    this.socket.on('end', () => this.onClientDisconnected());
  }

// callback for when a client disconnects
onClientDisconnected() {
  // tell any listeners that we have disconnected
  this.emit('end', this);
}
```

```
// callback for when a client sends us some data
onClientData(message) {

    // trim the data so that there are no empty spaces or line
    breaks etc
    var data = message.trim();

    console.log(`${this.clientName} says: ${data}`);

  }

}

module.exports = Client;
```

Like the GameServer class, the Client class has a constructor and it also takes in two arguments. But unlike that, here the two arguments that the Client class constructor takes are an id and the socket. The GameServer will pass on these two values to the new Client object when it is created. The Client stores the id and the socket and initializes some default values. The room variable, which is set to lobby when a Client is created, is an arbitrary string value that we will use later to determine where the player currently is. The currentGameID variable will eventually contain a unique id for a game the player is in. We then go on to set two listeners for the on data and on end events for the socket object. The onClientData function is called with the data that is sent to the socket. We will trim the incoming data and print it out onto the console along with our clientName. When a client closes the connection, the onClientDisconnected function is called. This emits an end event, passing along the Client object as an argument to the callback.

Now that we have seen that the Client class holds the socket object, meta-information about the client, and listeners to listen to new data coming in as well as handling the socket closing, we can return to the GameServer class and continue to explore what happens when a new client joins in.

```
// set the encoding for data on this socket to text
socket.setEncoding('utf8');
```

```
// generate a client id
var clientID = getRandomID();
```

```
// create a new client
var client = new Client(clientID, socket);
```

As soon as a new socket connection established, our server's onClientConnected() function is called. The first action that we take is to set the socket's encoding to utf8 like we saw in Chapter 5. After this, we create a unique identifier for the client using the built-in crypto module in NodeJS. For this game, we will simply use random bytes of data generated by the crypto.randomBytes() function. The getRandomID() function will return an id that will be unique for each player's session. Once we have an id, we will go ahead and use it along with the socket object to create a new Client object.

Tip   A universally unique identifier (or UUID, for short) is a 128-bit number used to identify objects or information in a computer system. In all our examples, we generate a 128-bit (16 bytes) number to be used as an id for our clients. In the future, it would be a good idea to explore how to generate valid UUIDs for the same.

```
// log to console
console.log(`New client connected: ${client.clientName}`);
```

```
// welcome message with client id
socket.write(JSON.stringify(["hello", client.id]));
```

Once the new Client object is created, we will log a message onto the server's console with the client's name. We then send a "hello" message along with the client's unique identifier as a JSON string. The client will receive the hello and understand it has made the right connection and can then look for the identifier and store it for future use.

```
// add client to our clients list
this.clients.push(client);

console.log(`client count: ${this.clients.length}`);

// clean up for the server when the client disconnects
client.on('end', (client) => this.
onClientDisconnected(client));
```

We then push the newly created client object into the clients array and print out to the server console the length of the array, effectively the number of clients connected to the server. Once this is done, we set up a listener for the client's end event. This listener will get called when any of the clients get disconnected.

```
onClientDisconnected(client) {
  console.log(`${client.clientName} has disconnected!`);

  // remove the client from our clients list once it has been
  disconnected!
  var c = this.getIndexWithID(this.clients, client.id);
  if(c != -1) {
    this.clients.splice(c, 1);
  }

  console.log(`client count: ${this.clients.length}`);
}
```

When a client disconnects, the end event is fired by the Client object, and the onClientDisconnected() function in the GameServer object gets

154

called as a result. First, we print a message onto the console saying that a client has disconnected, along with their name. We then get the index of client using their unique id from the client array and remove it using the arrays splice function. The getIndexWithID() function takes the id and uses the findIndex() method of the Array object that is passed to it to retrieve an index of the item (client, in this case) in the array. Once the Client object is removed, we print out the number of clients that are still connected to the server.

Let us run our server and try to connect to it and see what happens. Like before, navigate to the folder where your server is via the terminal or command prompt and run the app.js file using node.

```
# node app.js
```

Once you start the server you should see a message similar to what is given here.

```
Server started at 127.0.0.1:5836
```

Open up a new command prompt, type in the following, and hit enter. We will try to use telnet to connect to our server. If you do not have telnet installed on your computer and you are using Microsoft Windows, you can turn on telnet from the Control Panel (Control Panel\All Control Panel Items\Programs and Features) and navigate to a section called Programs and Features and then click on Turn Windows Features on and off to get a new window with a list of features that you can enable and disable. From this list enable Telnet Client and click ok. Now, the telnet application will be available for use from the command prompt. For more information on how to please check this link: https://kb.ctera.com/article/how-to-open-a-telnet-session-on-windows-7-or-windows-8-os-16.html. Alternatively you can try a telnet client like PuTTY as well https://www.chiark.greenend.org.uk/~sgtatham/putty/

```
# telnet 127.0.0.1 5836
```

Once the connection is established you should see a positive response in the telnet application like what is shown here:

```
["hello","9a78fcc36287ec5f84f7bc238c955136"]
```

At the same time, in the previous terminal window, you will notice that a new connection has been established in the server.

```
New client connected:
9a78fcc36287ec5f84f7bc238c955136:127.0.0.1:58055
client count: 1
```

If we open a new telnet window from another terminal or command prompt and connect to the server, we see that a new client has joined in and has a unique identifier assigned to it as well as the client count increased by 1.

```
Server started at 127.0.0.1:5836
New client connected:
9a78fcc36287ec5f84f7bc238c955136:127.0.0.1:58055
client count: 1
New client connected:
8b78a6cda2c17720afa8d26b893e63e2:127.0.0.1:59481
client count: 2
```

If you type in some text in the telnet client and hit enter, you will see a response in the server console like what is shown here:

```
8b78a6cda2c17720afa8d26b893e63e2:127.0.0.1:59481 says: awesome
```

From the previous section about our `Client` class, you will remember that whenever the client receives any data, it immediately prints it to the console. If we close the two telnet clients we can see that the client responds by showing the appropriate message and client count.

```
8b78a6cda2c17720afa8d26b893e63e2:127.0.0.1:59481 has
disconnected!
client count: 1
9a78fcc36287ec5f84f7bc238c955136:127.0.0.1:58055 has
disconnected!
client count: 0
```

Now that our server can manage clients (connecting, disconnecting, and sending messages), let us expand on this to add new features to the server as well as create the game client in GameMaker Studio.

Starting the Game Client in GameMaker Studio

In this section we will focus on creating the game client in GameMaker Studio and connecting it to the server and receiving the hello message.

We will start by creating a new project. The first thing we will do is to rename the existing room to `rmStart` and set room size to 1280 by 960 pixels. We will then import a background image by dragging it into the main window and creating a sprite from it; name this `sprBgTitle`. In the room, set the sprite as the image for the background layer.

Next, we will create an object that will act as our network manager, which will connect, send, and receive data to and from the server. There will only be one network manager instance in the whole game; we will call it `objNetManager`. Make sure the instance of this object will be persistent by clicking and checking the option in the Object editor. We will add four variables to this object. Add one of type `Real` for the `socket` and `port`.

Set the value of socket to *-1* and the port to *5836*. Add another variable of type String for the address; we will name it the same and set its value to localhost. The fourth and last variable we will add is a simple String that will hold a connection status message called status. Set the value for status to "connecting." Once this is done, let us add a Create event for objNetManager. The Create event will contain a function call to a script that we will create in the next step.

```
nmConnect();
```

We will keep the nmConnect() function separate in a script so that in case we need to reconnect in the future, it can be as simple as a function call. Create a new script and rename it to nmConnect and add the code below as seen in Listing 6-4.

Listing 6-4. Script nmConnect, Sets Up the Networking

```
/// @function      nmConnect()
/// @description   Create a connection with the server.

with(objNetManager) {

        // tell gamemaker to timeout this connection if there
        is no response in 4000ms (4 seconds)
        network_set_config(network_config_connect_timeout, 4000);

        // tell gamemaker to use a non-blocking socket connection
        network_set_config(network_config_use_non_blocking_
        socket, 1);

        // create a socket connection
        socket = network_create_socket(network_socket_tcp);

        // connect to the remote socket
        network_connect_raw(socket, address, port);

}
```

We change the scope to the network manager object objNetManager so that when we connect to the server and receive data, that object's async networking event gets triggered. Just like in Chapter 5, we set up the network settings and create a socket. Once this is done and a connection is successfully established, we will receive our hello message along with the player id.

Listing 6-5. Async-Networking Event for objNetManager

```
/// @description Handle network messages

// get the type of network event that has happened
type = async_load[? "type"];

switch(type)
{
        // we have connected to the server
        case network_type_non_blocking_connect:

                // check if we actually succeeded in connecting
                to the server
                if(async_load[? "succeeded"] == 1) {
                        status = "connection successful";
                } else {
                        status = "connection failed!";
                }

                break;

        // handle data coming to this client
        case network_type_data:

                // getting the data from the buffer
                var data = "";
                var pos = buffer_tell(async_load[? "buffer"]);
```

```
            data += buffer_read(async_load[? "buffer"],
            buffer_text);

            status = data;

            break;

    // unhandled or unknown events.
    default:

            show_debug_message("uncaught network event!");

            break;
}
```

Like our last example from Chapter 5, once a connection is established, we set the status to a success or failure message. When the welcome message comes, we will gather the data and set the data to the status variable. For now, we will create some UI elements that can display this status text.

Let us create a simple object that can display text stored in a variable. Create a new object and rename it to objLabel. Add four variables: text of type String, left empty; color of type Color, with a value white ($FFFFFFFF); halign of type Expression, with a value fa_center; and valign of type Expression, with a value fa_middle. Once this is done, add a Draw event for objLabel and add the following code.

```
/// @description Draws the text using the halign, valign, color
and text properties of the object

draw_set_halign(halign);
draw_set_valign(valign);
draw_set_color(color);
draw_text(x, y, text);
```

Using the variables of objLabel, we will simply draw the text onto the instance's x- and y-coordinates. Now that we have a basic label object, let's use it as a parent of an object to create custom UI labels. Create a new object and rename it to objTextStatusConnecting. This object will show a message on screen with the status and data when it arrives. Add our *objLabel* as the parent to this object. Once this is done, add a Step event for objTextStatusConnecting and add the following line:

```
text = objNetManager.status;
```

With the above, whenever objNetManager's status variable changes, out text will also change. Drag and drop an instance of objTextStatusConnecting onto the room's Instances layer.

If the game server is not running and if we run the game at this point, you will see a *connecting* message that will remain for 4 seconds on the screen and then be replaced with a new message that says, *connection failed!* If our server was running, we would see the hello message onscreen along with the player id. We have successfully managed to connect with the server and receive messages from it. In the next section, we expand on this to format our data better as well as do matchmaking. All the code up to now can be found in the code for this chapter in a folder named Section 1, and the GameMaker Studio file can be found along with the same and is named gms2_ch06_01.yyz.

Updating Our Server: Organizing the Data

The first thing that we will do is to add a send method to our Client class so that we can conveniently use it to send data to each client specifically. Open Client.js, and add the new method as shown in Listing 6-6.

Listing 6-6. Client.js: Write Data to the Client

```
// write data to the open socket
send(data) {
  if(this.socket.writable) {
    this.socket.write(JSON.stringify(data));
  }
}
```

Now the server can call the `Client.send()` function with data to any of the clients connected to the server. The function makes sure the socket is writable and then and then writes the data after converting it into a JSON string.

Now that our clients have a send method, let's change the structure in which the data has been organized. At the moment, the data is a simple object containing two strings. Let us structure them in a way that they are more meaningful for us in all contexts we use them. In the `GameServer.js` file, as soon as the client is connected, we send out the hello message in the `onClientConnected()` function; let's change that to

```
client.send({type:"hello", data:client.id});
```

Instead of using `JSON.stringify()` with an array, we will manually construct an object using the object initializer, add properties, and set the values for the items. All our messages to and from the server will follow the same messaging format. The first property will always be `type`, which qualifies what kind of a message it is, followed by the `data` property, which will contain the actual data itself. If we start the server and then our game now, you will see that it shows our new data format. The updated JavaScript files for this section can be found in the code for this chapter in a sub-folder called Section 2/01.

Updating Our Client: Reading the Player ID and Storing It

Let's re-open our client in GameMaker Studio and navigate to the *objNetManager* object. After updating our server, we are receiving a JSON string containing the hello message, which holds the player's unique ID. When we receive this hello message, we will set a variable called connected to true as well as store the player ID into a variable called player_id. First, let's add these variables to the objNetManager object. Open the Variable definitions window in the Object editor and add two variables. The first is connected; change its type to Boolean, and leave its value unchecked. The second variable is player_id; change its type to String, and leave the value text box empty.

Once this is done, open the *Async-Networking* event and navigate to where we set the status. Here, we will decode the JSON data and use the mapped values individually, first to check what message we have received and then to use the data.

```
// decoding the data
var resultMap = json_decode(data);

// what type of message is it?
var msgType = resultMap[? "type"];

// if message type is - hello
if(msgType == "hello") {
        connected = true;
        player_id = string(resultMap[? "data"]);

        status ="message type: " + msgType + "\ndata: " +
        player_id;
}
```

Like before, we use the json_decode function to decode the JSON string and store the result in a ds_map. We then use the ds_map_find_value() function to get the value stored in the variable we named type. Once we find the type of the message that we have received and if it is a hello message, we will then go ahead and extract the value stored in the data variable. Once this is done, we will display it as part of the status. The GameMaker Studio file for this section can be found in the code for this chapter in a subfolder called Section 2/01 and is called gms2_ch06_02_01.yyz.

Updating Our Server: Matchmaking and the Game Class

Now that we can receive data, let's create a framework that will help us handle a player versus player match. We will call it the Game class. When the client tries to tell the player that it needs to start a new match, the server tries to find any other players that are already waiting in queue to play. If there are no players in the queue, we will wait for another player to join. Once there are at least two players in the queue, these two players are removed from this waiting list, and a new game object is created for them. The Game class will handle all game logic as well as keep all the game data synchronized between the two players. Let us start by creating the Game class.

Listing 6-7. Game.js: All Game Logic and Data Synchronization Happens in This Class

```
const EventEmitter = require('events');

module.exports = class Game extends EventEmitter {

  constructor(id, p1, p2) {
    super();
```

```javascript
    // game id
    this.id = id;

    // the players
    this.p1 = p1;
    this.p2 = p2;

    // setting some player properties
    this.p1.room = "game";
    this.p2.room = "game";
    this.p1.currentGameID = this.id;
    this.p2.currentGameID = this.id;

    // our current player, when the game starts is always
    player one!
    this.currentPlayer = this.p1;

    // a game over flag
    this.gameOver = false;

    // a flag to mark who won the game
    this.gameWinner = 0;

    this.broadcast({type: "game-start", data:this.state});
}

// broadcasts a message to both the players
broadcast(msg) {
  this.p1.send(msg);
  this.p2.send(msg);
}

// the current state of the game bits
get state() {
  return {
```

```
      "id": this.id,
      "currentPlayer": this.currentPlayer.id,
      "gameOver": this.gameOver,
      "gameWinner": this.gameWinner
    };
  }

  end() {
    this.gameEnded = true;
    this.emit('end', this);
  }

  cleanup() {
    // clean up if any
  }
}

module.exports = Game;
```

Like the Player class, the Game class will also inherit the EventEmitter class so that we can emit events for each of the messages we receive from the clients.

The constructor for the class takes an id for the game itself and the two players who will be playing against each other—the two clients. In the constructor, we set the game's id as well as some more properties for the clients. We set some more flags before broadcasting a game-start message along with the current state of the game to both the clients. The state property collates all the variables and flags we have set in one single call. The broadcast function uses the Client.send() function that we had created earlier to send out a message to both the clients.

The Game class also has an end() function and a cleanup() function that we will see being used later. The first one is to end the game and emit the End event in case a player drops off or decides to stop playing; and the

166

second one is a cleanup function that will reset some default variables and free up memory when a game ends. We will add these later when we revisit the Game class in detail.

Now that we have a barebones Games class up and running, let us go back to the GameServer class to receive requests from clients to start a game and match them with other players.

Let's open the Client.js file so that we can modify the onClientData() function, as shown in Listing 6-8.

Listing 6-8. Client.js: onClientData Function

```
// callback for when a client sends us some data
onClientData(message) {

  console.log(`${this.clientName} says: ${message.trim()}`);

  // trim the message and try parsing it, if it fails tell the
client.
  var data;
  try {
    data = JSON.parse(message.trim());
  } catch(e) {
    this.send("parseerror");
    return;
  }

  // client is requesting a match
  if(data.type === "find" && data.data === "match") {
    if(this.room == "lobby") {
      this.room = "wait";
      this.emit('match', this);
    }
  }
}
```

```
// client is quitting matchmaking or a game
if(data.type === "quit") {
  this.room = "lobby";
  this.emit('quit', this);
}
}
```

When we receive any new data, we trim it and then try to parse it using JSON.parse() to convert the JSON string into an object and store it in the data variable. If the parsing fails, we send a message back to the client and exit the function. If the parsing was successful, we then check if the data.type is set to find and the data.data is set to the String match. If we are in the lobby (and not in a game or waiting), then change our room to a waiting room, and emit an event called match. The GameServer will see that the client has requested a match and see if there are any players available. Apart from the match event, we also emit a quit event, just so that we can quit while we are doing matchmaking or while we are in the middle of a game.

Before we begin, we need to modify our GameServer.js file by adding a require statement to import the Game class we wrote previously.

```
const Game = require("./Game.js");
```

Once this is done, we need to modify the constructor of the GameServer class to accommodate a list of clients who are looking for matches, as well as a list of games that are currently active.

```
// all our clients
this.clients = [];

// a list of clients looking for a match
this.lookingForMatches = [];
```

In onClientConnected() add an event listener to listen to any match requests as well as any requests to end the match or requests for matchmaking. Let us now write a couple functions to handle all incoming match requests as well as cancellations.

```
// client is looking for a match
client.on('match', (client) => this.onMatchRequest(client));
// client cancelled matchmaking or ended a game
client.on('quit', (client) => this.onStopPlaying(client));
```

When a client requests a match, the first thing we do is to add them to a waiting list. We then check to see if the waiting list has more players. If there are no other players waiting in the list, we simply tell the player who joined to wait by sending them a message of type wait. If there are at least two players, we create a new game with a random id and two players from the list. Once a game object is created, it is pushed to the games array. We also add a listener to catch the End event on the game object. We then splice the array twice to remove these two players from the waiting list now that they are in a game session (see Listing 6-9).

Listing 6-9. GameServer.js: onMatchRequest Function

```
// client requests to be matched with another player
onMatchRequest(client) {
  this.lookingForMatches.push(client);

  if(this.lookingForMatches.length >= 2) {
    let gameID = this.getRandomID();
    this.games.push(new Game(gameID,this.lookingForMatches[0],
    this.lookingForMatches[1]));
    this.games[this.games.length-1].on('end',(game) => this.
    onGameEnd(game));

    this.lookingForMatches.splice(0,1);
```

```
  this.lookingForMatches.splice(0,1);

  return;
 }

 // if no matches are found at the moment, we ask the client
 to wait
 client.send({"type":"wait"});
}
```

If the player quits while the matchmaking is happening or when the player is in the middle of a game, we can simply send a quit message to the server and it will drop us back onto main screen. At the same time, if we were on the waiting list, we would remove the client from it, and if we were in the middle of a game, we would end that game and clean up as we should as seen below in Listing 6-10.

Listing 6-10. GameServer.js: onStopPlaying Function

```
// client requests to be matched with another player
onStopPlaying(client) {
  // if we quit while waiting for players then remove the
  client from the list
  let m = this.getIndexWithID(this.lookingForMatches, client.id);
  if(m != -1) {
    this.lookingForMatches.splice(m, 1);
  } else {
    // if we were not in the waiting list, then we may have
    been in a game
    let g = this.games[this.getIndexWithID(this.games, client.
    currentGameID)];
    g.end();
  }
}
```

This will work, but before we can test it, we need to make sure that the games that we create are successfully destroyed when a player quits the game. We will also need to handle the case where a player quits the game when they are waiting for another player to join. Thankfully for us, we have set up our client in a way that it will emit an End event when the connection is closed. Let's take this opportunity to clean up and handle both these cases. At the moment, the onClientDisconnected() function removes our player from the clients array; let us make the following changes, as seen below in Listing 6-11, so that we can handle a player quitting in the middle of a matchmaking session as well as a game.

Listing 6-11. GameServer.js: onClientDisconnected Function

```
onClientDisconnected(client) {
  console.log(`${client.clientName} has disconnected!`);

  // if we quit while waiting for players then remove the
  client from the list
  let m = this.getIndexWithID(this.lookingForMatches, client.id);
  if(m != -1) {
    this.lookingForMatches.splice(m, 1);
  }

  // if the client was quit while playing a game, notify other
player and end game
  if(client.room == "game") {
    let g = this.games[this.getIndexWithID(this.games, client.
    currentGameID)];
    g.end();
  }
}
```

```
// remove the client from our clients list once it has been
disconnected!
let c = this.getIndexWithID(this.clients, client.id);
if(c != -1) {
  this.clients.splice(c, 1);
}

console.log(`client count: ${this.clients.length}`);
}
```

If the player is in the middle of a matchmaking session, they will be added to the lookingForMatches array. We will look for the player using their id in the lookingForMatches array, and if we find a match, we'll remove them just like we removed them from the clients array.

In the next section, we check if the client is in a game. If they are in the middle of a game, we use the game ID to retrieve that game object and call the game object's end() function. The end function in the game class does two things currently: sets the gameEnded variable to true and emits an End event.

In the onMatchRequest() function earlier, we started listening to the game object's End event; let's write the onGameEnd() function that will handle this event when it gets called. There are three things we need to handle: the two players and the game. If the players are still connected when the game ends, we will move them back to the lobby and send a message to them with the data game-end, which will inform the client that the game has ended on the server. Once this is done, we will remove the game from the games array and remove listeners for the End event (see Listing 6-12).

Listing 6-12. GameServer.js: onGameEnd Event Handler

```
// when a game ends, if everyone is still connected, move them
back to the lobby
onGameEnd(game) {
  if(game.p1.socket.writable) {
    game.p1.room = "lobby";
    game.p1.send({type: "game-msg", data:"game-end"});
  } else {
    game.p1.room = "closed";
  }

  if(game.p2.socket.writable) {
    game.p2.room = "lobby";
    game.p2.send({type: "game-msg", data:"game-end"});
  } else {
    game.p2.room = "closed";
  }

  // remove the game from the games array and cleanup
  let i = this.getIndexWithID(this.games, game.id);
  var g = this.games.splice(i, 1)[0];
  g.removeAllListeners('end');
  g = null;

}
```

Let us go through all the things we have done in the previous section so that we have a clearer picture of all the code we just wrote. We started with writing our bare bones Game class, which takes two players, sets up the game, and sends the connected players the game's state information.

Next, we focused on getting messages from the player and seeing if they wanted to start a game and, if they did match up with others who wanted to play, starting a game using the Game class. Apart from the matching we also handled what happens if a player disconnects while the matchmaking is happening or when the game is running as well as cleaning up the list of players and games when a game ends.

Let us go ahead and test to see if this works like we intended using our telnet client. Start the server and make sure that two telnet instances are connected to the server. You should see a response similar to what is given here:

```
Server started at 127.0.0.1:5836
New client connected:
bed382d8df1ce674b642c8b7f6ea679d:127.0.0.1:60949
client count: 1
New client connected:
b49c1855d949cad8a203f6885a831ed9:127.0.0.1:60953
client count: 2
```

Now that there are two clients connected, let us move to one of the telnet clients and type in the following:

```
{"type": "find", "data":"match"}
```

As soon as you type this in and hit enter, you will see that the server has received the data and sent you a response.

```
{"type":"wait"}
```

Let's do the same for the second telnet client and see what happens.

```
{"id":"709d789c6ca6cc4698ffe9d3b522f3b2","currentPlayer":"b49c1
855d949cad8a203f6885a831ed9","gameOver":false,"gameWinner":0}
```

As soon as the second player joins, the wait is now over. A new game is created and the details of the game are sent to the players. If you close one of the telnet clients, the game end event is fired, the game is shut down, and the game-end message is sent to the remaining clients.

```
{"type":"game-msg","data":"game-end"}
```

Now that we know that the server is working correctly, it is time for us to integrate the same into our GameMaker Studio client. The updated JavaScript files for this section can be found in the code for this chapter in a subfolder called Section 2/02.

Updating Our Client: Starting a Game, Waiting for Players, and Joining a Game

Let us start by creating three rooms: one for the menu screen, one as a waiting room, and the other for the game. Let us rename them to rmMenu, rmWait, and rmGame. Once a new connection is established, we will move the player to rmMenu. In the rmMenu room, we will have a button that will send a request to the server to start finding a match for the player and also move the player to the room rmWait. Once the server finds a match and a game is started, the player is taken to the game. We will add a button to both rmWait and rmGame so that users can quit and go back to the menu.

The first thing we will do is to change rooms once we establish a new connection. As soon we receive the hello message and the player ID, we will change the room to the menu room as well as change the status text (see Listing 6-13).

Listing 6-13. Async-Networking Event for objNetManager

```
// if message type is - hello
if(msgType == "hello") {
        connected = true;
        player_id = string(resultMap[? "data"]);

        status ="Welcome to the game!\nyour player id is - " +
        player_id;

        // go to the main menu
        room_goto(rmMenu);
}
```

Before we can go any further, we need to write a function through which we can communicate with the server. So far we have been receiving messages but not sending any. Let us create a new script and call it nmSendMessage. Let us add the following lines of code as seen in Listing 6-14 to the nmSendMessage script.

Listing 6-14. nmSendMessage, Sends Messages to the Server As a JSON String

```
/// @function      nmSendMessage()
/// @description  Send a type of message to the server.

var _type = argument0;
var _data = argument1;

var _msgMap = ds_map_create();
ds_map_add(_msgMap, "type", _type);
ds_map_add(_msgMap, "data", _data);
var _msg = json_encode(_msgMap);
ds_map_destroy(_msgMap);

var _buff = buffer_create(string_length(_msg), buffer_grow, 1);
buffer_write(_buff, buffer_text, _msg);

with(objNetManager) {
        if(network_send_raw(socket, _buff, buffer_tell(_buff))
        > 0) {
                show_debug_message("Data Sent!");
        } else {
                show_debug_message("Sending Failed!");
        }
}

buffer_delete(_buff);
```

The nmSendMessage() function takes in two arguments: one for the type of message and the second for the actual data itself. The function makes a ds_map out of the data and uses the json_encode() function to convert the map into a string. We then create a buffer that can hold the string and then write the string into the buffer's memory. We then use the network_send_raw() function to send the data buffer to the server, using the objNetManager object. We then delete the buffer to clear the memory.

Now that we have the means to send a message to the server, let's do just that. In the rmMenu room, let's add a button that will send a message to the server, asking it to find a game for us. To do this, add a button in rmMenu and name it objBtnStartGame like we have done before. In the Left Released event of the button, we will call our nmSendMessage() function asking the server to "find" a "match." Once we send the message out, we change our status display text and move to the next room, which is rmWait, where we wait for other players to join (see Listing 6-15).

Listing 6-15. objBtnStartGame: Left Released Event

```
nmSendMessage("find", "match");
objNetManager.status = "Looking for players!";
room_goto(rmWait);
```

In the waiting room, let's add another button that lets us cancel the search for a match and drop us back to the main menu. Let us rename our button to objBtnCancelWait. In the button's Left Released, we simply do the same as we did with the last button. We can add the same button to our next room rmGame so as to stop a game and return to the main menu (see Listing 6-16).

Listing 6-16. objBtnCancelWait: Left Released Event

```
nmSendMessage("quit", "");
objNetManager.status = "Lets play!";
room_goto(rmMenu);
```

177

Let us add that last bit that will finally take us to the game. When the server finds a match, it will create a game for us and send us all the details. So, let us receive this new game information and move the player to the rmGame room (see Listing 6-17).

Listing 6-17. Extract from Async-Networking Event for objNetManager

```
// if message type is - hello
if(msgType == "game-start") {

        var gameState = resultMap[? "data"];

        status = json_encode(gameState);

        // go to the main menu
        room_goto(rmGame);
}
```

In the objNetManager object's Async-Networking event, let's wait and see if we get the game-start message with the state of the game. Once we receive it, we will simply move to the rmGame room and set a status message with the data we received. The data in our case is a ds_map itself, which we are converting to a JSON string for the sake of this example. In the future, we will use the same ds_map that holds the state of the game to change the state of the game's display for the client.

One last thing that we have to take care of is what the client should do when the game ends. When a game ends, the server sends out a message of type game-msg with the data game-end. When we receive that message from the server, we can stop our session and move the player back to the main menu (see Listing 6-18).

Listing 6-18. Extract from Async-Networking Event for objNetManager

```
// if message type is - game-msg
if(msgType == "game-msg") {
        var data = string(resultMap[? "data"]);
        if(data == "game-end") {
                status = "Your last game has ended";
                room_goto(rmMenu);
        }
}
```

We are now able to start a new session with our server through the client, get a unique id, start a game with another player, and end it successfully. Now that we have come full circle, our next step is to focus on the game itself. At this point, testing using telnet is possible but cumbersome. To make this process a whole lot easier, what we can do is to make an executable. You can compile and make an executable from the Build menu in the GameMaker Studio IDE. Once compiled, you can run two or more instances of your game, along with the GameMaker Studio IDE as well.

We have laid the groundwork for what is required for our game to successfully communicate with the server. In the next section we will expand on this foundation to create the core of our turn-based game. The GameMaker Studio file for this section can be found in the code for this chapter in a subfolder called Section 2/02 and is called gms2_ch06_02_02.yyz.

Updating Our Server: Building the Core Game Mechanics

Now that our base is set, our focus will be to build the core of the game. As we decided at the beginning of this chapter, once a game starts, in their turn, each player roll their die until they either roll a 1 or they decide to hold the current turn total. Let us start of by setting up some variables that will hold these values for both our clients. Add a `score` and `turnTotal` variables to the `Client` class as seen below in Listing 6-19.

Listing 6-19. Client.js: Add a Score and turnTotal to the Client Class's Constructor

```
// holds the player's turn total and score for a game
this.score = 0;
this.turnTotal = 0;
```

Now that our clients can hold their own score and current turn total, let us move on and update the `onClientData()` event handler function so it can receive more messages from the clients. Before we proceed, we will modify this function so that it can handle the data coming in a bit more gracefully. If any of the data coming in is not proper JSON, our JSON parser will throw an error. What we will do at the beginning of the function is to put the `JSON.parse()` function used on the incoming data inside a `try...catch` statement block. This will catch any parsing errors that may happen due to corrupt data coming in via the client, send a message to the client who sent the corrupt data, and exit the function.

Now let us look at how to handle the parsed data. At present, we only handle messages that request a match and the message received when the player quits. We will add three more conditions to handle different messages when we are in a game: *ready*, *roll*, and *hold*. As they suggest, the ready message is sent by the client when it is ready to start the game, and the roll message is sent when the client wants to roll their die. The hold message is sent when the client wants to hold their current turn total. Each message will emit a corresponding event so that our Game class can handle these requests successfully (see Listing 6-20).

Listing 6-20. Client.js: onClientData Function

```
// callback for when a client sends us some data
onClientData(message) {

  console.log(`${this.clientName} says: ${message.trim()}`);

  // trim the message and try parsing it, if it fails tell the
  client.
  var data;
  try {
    data = JSON.parse(message.trim());
  } catch(e) {
    this.send({"type": "error", "data":"parseerror"});
    return;
  }

  // client is requesting a match
  if(data.type === "find" && data.data === "match") {
    if(this.room == "lobby") {
      this.room = "wait";
      this.emit('match', this);
    }
  // client is quitting matchmaking or a game
  } else if(data.type === "quit") {
    this.room = "lobby";
    this.emit('quit', this);
  // ready to start the game
```

```
  } else if(data.type === "msg" && data.data === "ready") {
    if(this.room === "game") {
      this.emit('ready', this);
    }
  // if we are in the game and the client wants to roll
  } else if(data.type === "do" && data.data ==="roll") {
    if(this.room === "game") {
      console.log(this.clientName, data.type, data.data);
      this.emit('roll', this);
    }
  // if we are in the game and the client wants to hold the
  current turn total
  } else if(data.type === "do" && data.data ==="hold") {
    if(this.room === "game") {
      console.log(this.clientName, data.type, data.data);
      this.emit('hold', this);
    }
  }
}
```

Now that we have more events to listen to, let us update the Game class to listen as well as respond to these new events. To keep track of the player's current score and turn total and to see if the user is indeed ready to play this round, we will add some more new properties to the player and set their defaults. Apart from properties for both players, we keep track of who the current player is, if the game is over or not, who the winner of the game is, as well as the last rolled die value. We will keep track of these items and send them to the players as part of the game's state. In the Game's constructor, we will also start listening to the ready, roll, and hold events, for both the players. Once this is set, we will broadcast the game ready message to both the players (see Listing 6-21).

Listing 6-21. Game.js: Constructor-Add

```
constructor(id, p1, p2) {
  super();

  console.log("Creating game - " + id);
  // game id
  this.id = id;

  // the players
  this.p1 = p1;
  this.p2 = p2;

  // setting some player properties
  this.p1.room = "game";
  this.p1.currentGameID = this.id;
  this.p1.turnTotal = 0;
  this.p1.score = 0;
  this.readyP1 = false;

  this.p2.room = "game";
  this.p2.currentGameID = this.id;
  this.p2.turnTotal = 0;
  this.p2.score = 0;
  this.readyP2 = false;

  // our current player, when the game starts is always player one!
  this.currentPlayer = this.p1;

  // a game over flag
  this.gameOver = false;

  // a flag to mark who won the game
  this.gameWinner ="";
```

```
// our last die roll
this.lastRoll = 0;

// clients are ready
this.p1.on('ready', (client) => this.onPlayersReady(client));
this.p2.on('ready', (client) => this.onPlayersReady(client));

// client requested to do a die roll
this.p1.on('roll', (client) => this.onDoRoll(client));
this.p2.on('roll', (client) => this.onDoRoll(client));

// client requested to hold current turn total
this.p1.on('hold', (client) => this.onDoHold(client));
this.p2.on('hold', (client) => this.onDoHold(client));

    // ask the player's if they are ready
    this.broadcast({type: "game-ready", data:this.state});
}
```

The ready message consists of the initial state of the game as well, which tell the players who is going first, and the clients are required to send a ready message back. Once the ready message comes back from both the players to the onPlayersReady() function, the game gets on the way (see Listing 6-22).

Listing 6-22. Game.js: onPlayersReady Function

```
// players are ready!
onPlayersReady(client) {
  if(client.id === this.p1.id) {
    this.readyP1 = true;
  }

  if(client.id === this.p2.id) {
    this.readyP2 = true;
  }
```

```
// are the players ready?
this.playersReady = (this.readyP1 && this.readyP2);

// check if both players have sent in a ready signal
if(this.playersReady) {
  this.playersReady = false;
  this.readyP1 = false;
  this.readyP2 = false;
  this.broadcast({type: "game-start", data:this.state});
  }
}
```

Once both players have sent a ready message to the server, the game broadcasts a *game-start* message along with the state of the game. Now that the game has started, we can wait for the clients to roll a die or hold their turn total (see Listing 6-23).

The onDoRoll() and onDoHold() functions are very similar. While one handles the roll, the other handles the hold. Both handle in-game action requests from the clients. In the onDoRoll() function, we pick a random number between 1 and 6, inclusive, and if the number is not 1, we add it to the turn total; if it is 1, then we clear the client's turn total to 0 and switch the current player. This means if it was player one's turn and they rolled a 1, we set their turnTotal variable to 0 and then set the currentPlayer value to player two. We then broadcast a game-update message to both clients. The onDoHold() works in a similar way, but instead of rolling the die, we simply take the turn total and add it to the player's score variable and then switch players. If the current player's score is more than or equal to 100, then we set that player as the gameWinner and set the gameOver flag to true, signaling to all the clients that the game is now over, and a winner has been selected. The game's state property will reflect this when it is broadcasted to the clients. Once this is done, we call the Game class's end() function to emit the end event as well as remove users and event listeners

and do general clean-up for the game. You will also notice that the end()
function is called using a setTimeout() function with a delay of 1000
milliseconds. This is so that the clients have enough time to process our
previous broadcast.

Listing 6-23. Game.js: Adding Event Handlers for Roll and Hold for
Both Players

```
// callback handles client roll die requests
onDoRoll(client) {
  this.lastRoll = this.roll();

  if(this.currentPlayer == this.p1) {
    if(this.lastRoll == 1) {
      this.currentPlayer = this.p2;
      this.p1.turnTotal = 0;
    } else {
      this.p1.turnTotal += this.lastRoll;
    }
  } else {
    if(this.lastRoll == 1) {
      this.currentPlayer = this.p1;
      this.p2.turnTotal = 0;
    } else {
      this.p2.turnTotal += this.lastRoll;
    }
  }

  this.broadcast({type: "game-update", data:this.state});
}
```

```
// callback handles client hold requests
onDoHold(client) {

  if(this.currentPlayer == this.p1) {
    this.p1.score += this.p1.turnTotal;
    this.p1.turnTotal = 0;

    if(this.p1.score >= 100) {
      this.gameWinner = this.p1.id;
      this.gameOver = true;
    } else {
      this.currentPlayer = this.p2;
    }
  } else {
    this.p2.score += this.p2.turnTotal;
    this.p2.turnTotal = 0;

    if(this.p2.score >= 100) {
      this.gameWinner = this.p2.id;
      this.gameOver = true;
    } else {
      this.currentPlayer = this.p1;
    }
  }

  this.broadcast({type: "game-update", data:this.state});

  if(this.gameOver) {
    console.log("Ending game: " + this.id);
    // end the game and send end game messages after a second.
    setTimeout(() => this.end(), 1000);
  }
}
```

```
// roll a 1d6
roll() {
  return Math.floor((Math.random()*6)+1);
}
// broadcasts a message to both the players
broadcast(msg) {
  console.log("game " + this.id + " says: " + JSON.
  stringify(msg))
  this.p1.send(msg);
  this.p2.send(msg);
}

// the current state of the game bits
get state() {
  return {
    "id": this.id,
    "currentPlayer": this.currentPlayer.id,
    "gameOver": this.gameOver,
    "gameWinner": this.gameWinner,
    "p1TurnTotal": this.p1.turnTotal,
    "p2TurnTotal": this.p2.turnTotal,
    "p1Score": this.p1.score,
    "p2Score": this.p2.score,
    "lastRoll": this.lastRoll
  };
}
```

Once the game ends, the end() function is called, we emit the end event, and we continue to do clean up. Clean up entails setting all player variables to default values as well as removing the listeners associated with the clients and the game (see Listing 6-24).

Listing 6-24. Game.js: The End and Cleanup Functions

```
end() {
  this.gameEnded = true;
  console.log("Emitting end event!");
  this.emit('end', this);
  this.cleanup();
}

cleanup() {
  // clean up if any
  this.p1.turnTotal = 0;
  this.p1.score = 0;
  this.p2.turnTotal = 0;
  this.p2.score = 0;

  // clients are ready
  this.p1.removeAllListeners('ready');
  this.p2.removeAllListeners('ready');

  // client requested to do a die roll
  this.p1.removeAllListeners('roll');
  this.p2.removeAllListeners('roll');

  // client requested to hold current turn total
  this.p1.removeAllListeners('hold');
  this.p2.removeAllListeners('hold');

  console.log("Cleanup complete!");
}
```

The Game along with its onDoRoll() and onDoHold() functions form the core, and our work so far provides the scaffolding to hold it all together. Now that we have our game logic in place, let us add the core game screens to our GameMaker Studio clients. The updated JavaScript files for this section can be found in the code for this chapter in a subfolder called Section 3/01.

Updating Our Client: The Game Screen

At this moment, our game gets started, but only a status message with the data that comes in from the server at the start of the game is visible. We will parse that state information and use it to show the status of the game, as well as add buttons for the two commands that our clients require: roll and hold. Make sure the buttons you add have a mechanism in place to enable and disable them by setting an enable variable to true or false. We don't need our users to be pressing the buttons when they are not supposed to, like when it is not their turn.

But first, let us parse the game state information a little better. The game server sends the following state information as seen below in Listing 6-25 each time a new game starts or when the player does an action.

Listing 6-25. Game State Information From the Server

```
{
  "currentPlayer": "cee1c2c44aec26513c637a0164eace55",
  "gameOver": 0.000000,
  "gameWinner": "",
  "id": "aae2f15a32c6893e9b392d4818f430a4",
  "lastRoll": 0.000000,
  "p1Score": 0.000000,
  "p1TurnTotal": 0.000000,
  "p2Score": 0.000000,
  "p2TurnTotal": 0.000000
}
```

The state information tells us the ID for the current player and if it is game over or not. If it is game over, then we can find out who the winner is. It also tells us the last rolled die value, both players' scores, as well as turn total.

Our first objective would be to determine if we are player one or player two. As soon as the first set of information comes in, the first person to start the game is always treated as player one by our server. So here, the currentPlayer variable will let us know if we are the first player or not.

Listing 6-26. objNetHandler: Async–Networking, Game Is Ready to Start

```
// if message type is - game-ready
if(msgType == "game-ready") {
        status ="Starting game; waiting for everyone to join.";

        // go to the main menu
        room_goto(rmGame);
}
```

Once the game is ready to start, the server sends the game-ready message. As soon as we receive the message, we move our player from the waiting room to the game room (see Listing 6-26). In the game room's (rmGame) creation code, we send a message to the server telling it we have moved to the game room and we are ready to start (see Listing 6-27).

Listing 6-27. rmGame: Room Creation Code

```
nmSendMessage("msg", "ready");
```

Once the game is underway and the players are ready, the server sends the game-start message to the client. To handle this new incoming message, we have to check for the incoming message type and its data. Open up objNetManager and navigate to the Async-Networking event.

Here we will check if the msgType is game-start; if it is, we will compare the current player's ID stored in currentPlayer with our *ID* to determine if we are the first player or the second one. We set two new variables to the objNetManager object, player_position, and opponent_position after determining which player we are. If we are player one, the player_position variable will be p1 and opponent_position will be p2; otherwise, it is the other way around. We do so to access the current player's score and turn total from the game state data sent to us. If it is our turn, we will also enable the objBtnRollDie and objBtnHold buttons (see Listing 6-28). Let's add one more variable that will keep track of whether our match is over or not. Add a Boolean type variable called match_over and set its value to false.

Listing 6-28. objNetHandler - Async - Networking - Game starting for the first time

```
// if message type is - game-start
if(msgType == "game-start") {
        var gameState = ds_map_find_value(resultMap,"data");

        match_over = false;

        show_debug_message(json_encode(gameState));

        if(ds_map_exists(gameState, "currentPlayer")) {
                if(gameState[? "currentPlayer"] == player_id) {
                        player_position = "p1";
                        opponent_position = "p2";
                        status = "It is your turn, Click the
                        roll button to roll the dice!";

                        objBtnRollDie.enabled = true;
                        objBtnHold.enabled = true;

                } else {
                        player_position = "p2";
```

```
              opponent_position = "p1";
              status = "It is your opponent's turn,
              please wait!";

              objBtnRollDie.enabled = false;
              objBtnHold.enabled = false;
         }
      }
}
```

Now that we can start the game, let us handle the game-update message sent by the player. The code in Listing 6-29 might seem intimidating, but it is very similar to how the code we have worked with above in Listing 6-28 works. What it does extra is to look through the state data sent to it and use that to show the right information. Let us take a closer look.

Listing 6-29. objNetHandler: Async–Networking, Game Update Message Sent Every Time a Player Takes a Turn

```
// if message type is - game-update
if(msgType == "game-update") {
  var gameState = ds_map_find_value(resultMap,"data");

  show_debug_message(json_encode(gameState));

  var msg = "";

  // is the game over?
  if(gameState[? "gameOver"]) {

    match_over  = true;

    // did you win?
    if(gameState[? "gameWinner"] == player_id) {
      msg = "You have won the match!\n";
```

```
      msg += "you beat your opponent with a score of " +
      string(gameState[? player_position+"Score"]) + " against
      " + string(gameState[? opponent_position+"Score"]));
    } else {
      msg = "You lost the match!\n";
      msg += "your opponent beat you with a score of " +
      string(gameState[? opponent_position+"Score"]) + "
      against " + string(gameState[? player_position+"Score"]));
    }

    objBtnRollDie.enabled = false;
    objBtnHold.enabled = false;

  } else {

    if(gameState[? "currentPlayer"] == player_id) {

      if(gameState[? "lastRoll"] == 1) {
        msg = "Your opponent rolled a 1 and ended their
        turn\n";
      } else {
        if(string(gameState[? player_position+"TurnTotal"]) ==
        "0") {
        msg = "Your opponent decided to hold!\n";
        } else {
        msg = "You rolled a " + string(gameState[? "lastRoll"])
        + "\n";
        }
        msg = "You rolled a " + string(gameState[? "lastRoll"])
        + "\n";
      }
```

```
msg += "It is your turn.\n\n"
msg += "Your score is " + string(gameState[? player_
position+"Score"]) + " and your Turn total is "  +
string(gameState[? player_position+"TurnTotal"]) + "\n\n";
msg += "Your score is " + string(gameState[? player_
position+"Score"]) + " - Your opponent's score is " +
string(gameState[? opponent_position+"Score"]);

objBtnRollDie.enabled = true;
objBtnHold.enabled = true;
} else {
  if(gameState[? "lastRoll"] == 1) {
    msg = "You rolled a 1 and ended your turn\n";
  } else {
      if(string(gameState[? opponent_
      position+"TurnTotal"]) == "0") {
    msg = "Your turn has ended!\n";
      } else {
    msg = "Your opponent rolled a " + string(gameState[?
    "lastRoll"]) + "\n";
      }
·}
  msg += "Your opponent is playing!!\n\n";
  msg += "Their score is " + string(gameState[? opponent_
position+"Score"]) + " and their Turn total is "  +
string(gameState[? opponent_position+"TurnTotal"]) + "\n\n";
  msg += "Your score is " + string(gameState[? player_
position+"Score"]) + " - Your opponent's score is " +
string(gameState[? opponent_position+"Score"]);
```

```
    objBtnRollDie.enabled = false;
    objBtnHold.enabled = false;
  }

 }
 status = msg;
}
```

Once we parse the data from the server, we check the state to see if the game is over or not. If the game is over, we continue and check if we won the game. If we did, then we display a message with our winning score. If we lost the game, we show a similar message with the losing score. If the game is not over and the last rolled value is not 1, then we display our current die roll, score, and turn total, and enable the buttons so we can roll or hold. If we had rolled a 1 in our previous turn, our turn would have ended and now it would be the opponent's turn, where we display their current die roll value, score, and turn total as well as disable our buttons (see Listing 6-30).

Now that we can show the game's state information and we can roll and hold our value, we have a complete game in place. What is left is to end the game when a player wins and take us to the main menu room.

Listing 6-30. objNetHandler: Async–Networking, Handling Game-End Message

```
// if message type is - game-msg
if(msgType == "game-msg") {
        var data = string(ds_map_find_value(resultMap,"data"));
        show_debug_message("We've got a game message from the
        server! - " + data);

        if(data == "game-end") {
                show_debug_message("Ending game!");
                player_position = "";
```

```
opponent_position = "";
if(!match_over) {
        status = "Your opponent has left the
        match!\nPlease click the button below
        to find another player.";
        match_over = true;
}
room_goto(rmMenu);
    }
}
```

Once we get the game-end message, we set the player_position and opponent_position instance variables to their default values and take the player back to the main menu room. The GameMaker Studio file for this section can be found in the code for this chapter in a subfolder called Section 3/01 and is called gms2_ch06_03_01.yyz.

We now have a playable die rolling game that is ready to go live after some polish. Try to create an executable for your game and try playing with two instances of the same game running. You now have a basic turn-based multiplayer in your hands. Now that the gameplay elements are in place, what remains is to polish the game, update the interface, add sound effects and music, and finally host our server online so we can play with our friends.

Index

A, B, C

Control flow
    break statement, 42
    continue statement, 42
    do...until loop, 36–37
    elseif statement, 27
    else statement, 27
    exit statement, 42–43
    for loop, 37–38
    if statement, 27
    keyboard_check()
        function, 28–29
    key constant, 28–29
    objSpawnner, 34
    operators
        differences, 31
        equality operator (==), 30–31
        inequality operator (!=), 30–31
        object editor, 32
        step event, 30–31
    repeat loop
        enemy spawner script, 35
        instance_create_layer(), 35
        irandom_range()
            functions, 34
        objSpawner, 34, 36

switch statement
    break statement, 40
    clubbing conditions, 40
    show_debug_message()
        function, 42
    structure, 40
while loop, 36–37
with construction, 38–39
createServer() function, 105
crypto.randomBytes()
    function, 153

D

Die roller server
    Async-Networking event, 137
    buffers, 136
    getting data
        Async-Networking
            event, 137–139
        buffer, 140
        network_type_data
            event, 139
    GMS, 127
    JSON string, 141
    left-released event, 135
    modify server, 125

© Yadu Rajiv 2018
Y. Rajiv, *Developing Turn-Based Multiplayer Games*,
https://doi.org/10.1007/978-1-4842-3861-5

Y, Z

Printed in the United States
By Bookmasters